# SANTA BARBARA

# KNOW-
# IT-ALL

## A GUIDE TO EVERYTHING
## THAT MATTERS

### MICHAEL CERVIN

Copyright © 2018, Reedy Press, LLC
All rights reserved.
Reedy Press
PO Box 5131
St. Louis, MO 63139
www.reedypress.com

Library of Congress Control Number: 2017958843
ISBN: 9781681061375

Printed in the United States of America
18 19 20 21 22    5 4 3 2 1

# Why did I buy this book?

**Short answer:** I'm not sure.

**Long answer:** Because you're a smart, savvy traveler who doesn't want useless information—"suggestions" about where to eat and what to do that haven't been fully vetted by the author. And, you don't like wasting your valuable time and money on activities better suited to busloads of wide-eyed tourists with cheap cameras. You want to maximize your time, avoid the tourist traps and tedium, get forthright opinions, and finish your visit by saying, "That was awesome." All good?

# How this book works

## First, it's honest.

There's no glossing over lame places to visit and making them sound somehow superlative using ornamental verbiage (kinda like that). Something is either worth visiting or it isn't. We skip the mediocre and seek out the exceptional experiences that truly reflect where you are. You can get average anywhere. We'll tell you if a restaurant has great food but lousy service. We'll inform you of the ridiculous policies enacted by the local government so you don't get a ticket. We'll tell you what places aren't safe to visit after certain hours. Travel books should be fun to read, so we'll fill ours with witty comments and observations, never forgetting that travel should be educational *and* entertaining.

## Second, it's intuitive.

Listings of what to do and where to eat and stay are organized under the heading of each particular community (everything in the City of Santa Barbara is listed there, everything in Solvang is in that section, etc.). We simplify the process by listing just four sub-sections for each town: Do, Eat and Drink, Shop, and Stay. We list everything in alphabetical order.

---

Sights to see, things to do, festivals, museums and galleries—you know, all that stuff. We list only the full adult price. Yes, many places offer discounts for seniors, teenagers and kids, active members of the military, people with cats, folks who wear glasses, parents with no middle name . . . any number of categories. We don't give every specific because these things change, and we don't want you getting mad at us because the book says one price and you're charged a different price when you show up. Everything is as up to date as possible, but nothing is perfect.

## Eat AND Drink

Listings are in alphabetical order by type of cuisine, not by ranking, so they're easier to find. We don't usually list the opening hours, because honestly they change a lot and some take nearly a page to explain. We list the website, address, and phone number, in that order. We think you're smart enough to find out how late a bar is open, or whether that restaurant you want to try is closed on Mondays. Many of these places have websites and Facebook pages that you can look up on your phone. For restaurant service we list breakfast, lunch, and dinner as B, L, D. We use the $ symbol if the average meal is under $15, $$ for $15 to $25, and $$$ for meals over that. We do not list chain restaurants—yes, there are a few good ones—because we assume you came to Santa Barbara to discover what makes this place unique, not to eat at the same restaurant you have in your own town.

From the under-the-radar stores to the offbeat shops, we focus on stuff you might actually buy, as well as stores that are helpful for travelers or that reflect exactly where you are. We don't do chains: you don't need a travel maven to find Baby Gap.

Do we really need to explain this? We divide this into three categories: I'm on a Budget, Life Is Pretty Good, and I Just Won the Lottery. Enough said.

---

## Third

We don't do itineraries. "One Day Wonders" or things like "If You Only Have Three Days," aren't for us. Whether you're in town for one day, three days, or a week, how can we possibly know how you want to spend your time? We also don't create lists and then write something as banal as "watch the sunset." We figure you'll make your own list of what you want to do. Honestly, "people watching" *is* free, but it's free on your street corner, too.

## Fourth

We don't list "highlights." We also don't list "must sees," and "author favorites" because, if it's in this book, it's already what you need to know and where you need to eat and visit. And yes, everything, and I mean *everything*, has been personally vetted, meaning I've eaten, stayed, or shopped there. It's about price being commensurate with quality. We seek the coolest, most fun, and oddest things we can find. We have no agenda, we get no kickbacks for listing anything in our books, and unlike mainstream travel books we don't have page counts. That means we don't have to list twenty-five hotels; we list only the ones we like and think you'll love. And, most importantly, we tell you *why* you should consider a restaurant, bar, hotel, or site.

## Fifth

Historical context matters. Every city, town, and burg is important to your experience, so we always include some of it. Besides, half the time it's just so strange that you can't make this stuff up, so please read it. We also include Weird and Trivial . . . But True, a short piece with factoids, trivia, and other useless information about each place so you can impress your friends and sound like a smarty-pants.

## Sixth

There is no sixth category. We just like round numbers.

# TABLE OF CONTENTS

# SANTA BARBARA

## INTRO

## DO

## EAT AND DRINK

# CARPINTERIA, MONTECITO, AND SUMMERLAND

## EAT AND DRINK

## SHOP

## STAY

## OUTRO

# SOLVANG

## INTRO

## DO

# SANTA YNEZ AND SANTA MARIA VALLEY/WINE COUNTRY

# ACKNOWLEDGMENTS

Let's be honest, any book is a hassle to write, especially a travel book. Oh, sure, it all sounds glamorous and devil-may-care, as if I have nothing to do but wander about and eat and drink and stay in nice places, experience cool things, and have everyone be really, really friendly to me. That's absolute fantasy, my friends (except the part where I have nothing to do but wander about and eat and drink and stay in nice places, experience cool things, and have everyone be really, really friendly to me).

That aside, these people have been invaluable to the creation of this book, and I thank them for their input and time.

Kathy Gruver has been immensely helpful with stellar ideas to make this book even better than I thought it was.

Thanks also to AVW for providing me opportunities that, unbeknownst to either of us, built the foundation for this book.

Special thanks also to the Santa Barbara Convention and Visitors Bureau, the Solvang Conference and Visitors Bureau, and Laura Klath of Mariah Marketing for their insights.

Thanks as well to the family at Reedy Press for their support and willingness to consider a weird travel book like this one and for their undying focus on what small-town America gives back.

On a personal note, I hope this book inspires others to reach for their dreams and turn those wishes into reality. Life is a series of choices. When I first moved to Santa Barbara, I had an interview for a traditional job, which I thankfully didn't get. Sometimes when we're told no it causes us to pivot and look into something new. I wrote a poem about that interview, which was originally published in the literary journal of the University of New Orleans, *Bayou*. It's also in my book of poetry, *Generous Fiction*, and I include it here because, in many ways, it helped lay the foundation for this book.

## THE INTERVIEW

*If you squint hard enough she looks like Eva Braun.*
*Her hair in a bun, tightly coiled*
*ready to strike with dreadful rapidity.*

*She does not wear a wedding ring—*
*perhaps she killed her husband*
*or,*
*perhaps he killed himself.*

*The office lacks ventilation,*
*it seems like a trick,*
*though I do not fidget in my chair.*

*My tie hangs carelessly about my shirt,*
*too common for her tastes,*
*and now she tightens the noose.*

*Her hand outstretched, nails like talons,*
*I negotiate around them grasping the handshake*
*which tells me to get lost.*

*An African violet sits dormant on her desk.*
*I comment, trying to bond,*
*hoping to recover the fumble, but as there is no flower left,*
*it is my turn to go.*

# ABOUT THE AUTHOR

Michael Cervin is a wine, food, and travel writer and the author of four Moon travel books specific to the California Central Coast. He was a contributing travel writer and restaurant reviewer for the *Santa Barbara News-Press* for eight years. He contributes to diverse publications, including Forbes Travel Guides, *The Hollywood Reporter*, *The Robb Report*, *Decanter* (London), *Fine Wine & Liquor* (China), *Old Liquors Magazine* (the Netherlands), *Whiskey Reviewer*, *Wine Enthusiast*, *Wine & Spirits*, *The Tasting Panel*, *Skywest*, Gayot.com, IntoWine.com, *Arroyo Monthly*, the *Ventura County Reporter*, and more than a hundred others.

As a professional wine and spirits judge, he has judged various competitions, including the Best of Vinho Verde Awards in Portugal, the Taste of Rum Festival in Puerto Rico, the Global Bottled Water Awards in Prague, the Critics Challenge Wine Competition, the California State Fair Wine Competition, the Central Coast Wine Competition, the San Francisco International Wine Competition, the San Diego International Wine Competition, the Berkeley Springs International Water Tasting, and a host of other professional and charity events.

His speaking credits include the Golden Headwater Protection Summit in Beijing; GBWA in Prague; the Los

Angeles Travel and Adventure Show; the San Diego Travel and Adventure Show; the Wine Tourism Conference; Berkeley Springs International Water Tasting; the Central Coast Book and Author Festival; the Bay Area Travel and Adventure Show; the International Food, Wine, and Travel Writers Association; the North Coast Wine Industry Expo; and others.

## MICHAEL CERVIN'S OTHER BOOKS

- *Our World of Water: The Good, the Bad, and the Ugly of Earth's Most Critical Resource*
- *Generous Fiction* (poetry)
- *Blunted by Lunacy* (short stories)
- *California Road Trip*
- *California Wine Country*
- *Spotlight: Cambria and San Simeon*
- *Santa Barbara and the Central Coast*

## MICHAEL CERVIN'S BLOGS

- *Cervin's Central Coast* (CervinsCentralCoast.blogspot.com) focuses exclusively on the Central Coast, including Ventura, Santa Barbara, San Luis Obispo, and Monterey.
- *Exploracation* (exploracation.blogspot.com) is a global travel blog with articles about Austria, Crete, China, Santa Fe, Ukraine, Nova Scotia, Easter Island, and a whole bunch of other places he's traveled to.
- *Boozehound* (www.boozehoundz.blogspot.com) is all things booze, from wine and spirits and beer to books about booze, tasting events, and more.
- *This World of Water* (ThisWorldofWater.blogspot.com) covers water issues, such as bottled water, healthy hydration, water policy, wars, and more. This book is a call to respect our water.

# SANTA BARBARA

Santa Barbara is both a city and county defined geo-graphically by the Santa Ynez mountain range, which divides the southern beach portions of Santa Barbara, Carpinteria, Montecito, and Goleta from their northern neighbors of Solvang, Santa Maria, Santa Ynez, Buellton, Los Olivos, and Lompoc. And let's be honest . . . that's not a funny way to start a humorous travel book.

When folks think of Santa Barbara, they tend to think of the beach, the Spanish architecture, and the wine industry. They also think that we who live here have little else to do but tan ourselves and eat local lobster while guzzling our famous chardonnay. That's only partially correct—my tan is incomplete. The county contains a mere 450,000 souls, and while the media image of sun-drenched Santa Barbara's red-tiled roofs sounds cool, the county is an agri-cultural workhorse and an international tourist destination.

*A Know-It-All view of Santa Barbara*

1

A small shelf sandwiched between the Los Padres National Forest and the Pacific Ocean, the city of Santa Barbara appears to be suspended in time. But this town of roughly 120,000 people is fiercely proud of its cultural heritage, and Santa Barbara has a history extending back to when the Chumash people inhabited this area more than 10,000 years ago. Limiting a Santa Barbara visit to the oceanfront and State Street—the usual suspects for most tourists—would be like ignoring part of your family . . . well, except for that really weird uncle.

Yes, there is the shopping, the wine industry, the Spanish architecture that dominates the region, and a laid-back vibe inspired by endless waves and eternal sunshine. But there is also a wealth of physical activities. The Rincon is a favorite surf spot, but surfers dot the waters everywhere, and attending a "board meeting" is quite common. North County differs dramatically from the beach portion: there are the beautiful, rugged mountains and lots of agriculture, meaning lots of fields of planted things. The Western history of North County is still visible—cowboys still roam, and so do the cattle. Santa Barbara has such a wealth of cultural, architectural, and historical treasures that you'll need time to immerse yourself in the area. So? Start immersing.

## Hello, My Name Is . . .

The city of Santa Barbara has natural boundaries: the Los Padres National Forest on one side and the Pacific Ocean on the other. What's left is a reasonably small strip of land, and we try not to build too much on it. The city of Goleta is up the coast, and down the coast are the unincorporated areas of Montecito and Summerland and the city of Carpinteria, which abuts the county line with Ventura. Santa Barbara is defined by State Street, the main drag, which runs from the beach all through the downtown area. Twelve square blocks of history, restaurants, bars, and galleries are wrapped up in a pretty Spanish Mediterranean package. One of the main reasons people love it here is the uninterrupted views of the beach and mountains. You may not notice it at first, but we have no tall buildings. Our tallest building is just eight stories, built in 1924, and there's only one of those. The other thing you won't see are billboards along the freeway: Santa Barbara passed a sign ordinance in the 1920s, which affected billboards and even store signs around town. See, we really, really like our views.

The best time to visit is not summer. Sound counterintuitive? The ideal time to visit is from March to May, when everything is pristine and green after the mild winter rains. The Channel Islands are crisp and detailed, and the crowds are thin. Summer gets the May grey and June gloom, with marine layers that sometimes don't burn off until early afternoon, and the streets are as thick with people as with the consuming fog (how's that for poetic imagery). October through December is also a great time; sure, there's a higher chance of rain, but I can't tell you the number of Thanksgivings I've had where the family has been at the beach playing in the water, burning off the turkey, or driving home from the Christmas tree lot with an overpriced pine sticking out of my convertible.

## The Mystery of History

Technically, Santa Barbara, which was incorporated as a city in August 1850, is older than the state of California, which was admitted to the Union in September 1850. Okay, so it's just a month, but it does define the attitude of Santa Barbara—we are the center of the universe, thank you very much.

The Chumash people (pronounced "shoe-mash") were here for thousands of years, and then the Spanish ruled the region for several hundred years, and then Mexico kicked out Spain and took over, and then American know-how knew how to root out Mexico. So here we are now: an American town with Spanish-style architecture, lots of Mexican residents, and an Indian casino. That sounds about right.

Before Spanish explorers ever saw the coast of California, approximately 15,000 Chumash Indians lived between Malibu and San Luis Obispo and on the Channel Islands in self-sustaining, autonomous communities. They seemed pretty nice, and their language had eight different regional dialects. Cave paintings, artifacts, and petroglyphs are still scattered along the Central Coast, most notably the Painted Cave that the Chumash made to tell their stories. The Chumash were hunter-gatherers way before that became a knock-off term to refer to soccer moms and yuppie dads. They were a peaceful people: basket weavers and fishermen who were quite industrious in making boats (called tomols) by which they could paddle from the coast to Santa Cruz Island, about twenty-four miles away. I said paddle—not wind power or motor, paddle. You try doing that. I'm guessing the dudes were buff.

In 1542 Juan Rodríguez Cabrillo (I'm guessing not buff), an explorer guy from Portugal who was sailing for Spain, sailed into the Santa Barbara Channel and landed his ships at the Channel Islands, never setting foot on Santa Barbara soil. He hoisted up a Spanish flag and claimed the region for Spain. Because of this we gave him a street name, Cabrillo Boulevard, which fronts the ocean. That's all he really got out of the trip, seeing as how he died and was buried . . . well, somewhere in present-day California, most likely on one of the islands. Sebastián Vizcaíno, a cartographer (he who maketh maps) for the Duke of Monte Rey, was the one who landed in Santa Barbara on December 4, 1602, which happened to be the feast day of Saint Barbara (what, like they didn't plan that?), and put Santa Barbara on the map for the first time in history. The native Chumash people were relatively unimpressed with all this and had little to do with the Spanish until the arrival of missionaries in the mid-1700s. That's when things went south for the Chumash, though they didn't know it yet. They were nice, trusting people, and that backfired on them down the road.

Spain needed defensible positions along the coast. After all, any imperial power worries that someone will take its land. So it established the first presidio, a military fort, on April 21, 1782, in what is now downtown Santa Barbara; by all accounts it was a simple wooden structure. The formal version of the presidio (you can visit the replica) was constructed in 1784, followed by the construction of the mission in 1786. Spain ruled the region until the early 1820s, when Mexico fought for and won its independence from Spain. But Mexico's rule was short-lived, as the United States then declared war on Mexico in 1846 and took everything by force, using the idea of manifest destiny (you remember that from high school history?). Then we built ourselves a pleasant beach community.

By 1850 the California gold rush in Northern California's Sierra Nevada had lured thousands of people there. Those who failed miserably to strike it rich (the vast majority of them) left for other parts of California to seek their fortunes, and some of those immigrants and East Coast Americans (called "back-easters" by locals) ended up here in Santa Barbara, which was, at that time, nothing much of a town. But there was land and opportunity. The city has long had an enviable climate that drew people here for health reasons, and by the late 1880s Santa Barbara had developed a name for itself as a health resort. Business people seeking to capitalize on tourism potential promoted the healing environment of the area and the curative nature of the waters.

Many of the vast old estates built in Montecito were second homes for wealthy industrialists who could afford large parcels of land. But even then, although large and impressive hotels like the Potter and the Arlington catered to the elite, the city was still relatively small. The 1925 earthquake decimated parts of the city, and the decision was made to reinvent the city in the likeness of its original Spanish and Mexican influences for which Santa Barbara is known today. Now we are a world-class destination with a definable style (Spanish Colonial Revival) sitting on a small swath of land between the Pacific Ocean and the mountains. Not bad.

## Bullet Point History

- Native Chumash people fish and hang out, work on tan.
- Spanish sail by, decide they like beachfront property.
- Spanish guys build mission and fort, bring cattle, plant grapes.
- Mexico says "The heck with this," starts war with Spain.
- Spanish go bye-bye.
- US says, "The heck with Mexico, we want beachfront property," kicks them out.
- Wealthy Eastern whites flock here, buy up all the good land.
- Mother Nature triggers earthquake, Santa Barbara redefines itself.
- Oprah buys mega-estate.

## Weird and Trivial . . . But True!

ⓘ Elizabeth Short, known as the Black Dahlia, was arrested in Santa Barbara for underage drinking in 1943, four years before she was found murdered in Los Angeles and became the stuff of legend.

ⓘ Hidden Valley Ranch salad dressing was born in Santa Barbara and was named for Hidden Valley Ranch in rural Santa Barbara County. Steve Henson created the dressing recipe while living in Alaska before purchasing Hidden Valley Ranch. Cold Spring Tavern was the first restaurant to serve his dressing, and the brand was purchased in 1973 for $8 million. It's gone on to become America's most pop-ular salad dressing, and who doesn't dip their potato skins in ranch dressing?

ⓘ The very first Motel 6 opened in Santa Barbara in 1962, and it's still there at 443 Corona Del Mar, just a block from the beach. Six bucks a night was the going rate then. Now there are more than 1,000 locations nationwide, and the current rate in Santa Barbara tops $200.

ⓘ Tons of films, TV shows, and commercials have been shot in Santa Barbara. Between 1910 and 1921, the largest film studio in the world was located here; the only remain-ing part is at Chapala and Mission streets. It was called Flying A Studios. Just a few of the better-known movies shot here are *Sideways*, *Seabiscuit*, *It's Complicated*, and *Pirates of the Caribbean: At World's End*. *The Creature from the Black Lagoon* and *Friday the 13th* were shot at Zaca Lake in the Santa Ynez Valley. TV shows include *Monk*, *Top Chef*, and *The Bachelor*.

ⓘ Singer Katy Perry, who was born here, learned to dance at the Carrillo Recreation Center and sang at church. She went to Dos Pueblos High School (go DP!) and now is Santa Barbara's most well-known celebrity (aside from the part-timer known as Oprah), pulling in about $50 million in 2016 alone. Must be our weather.

ⓘ There is a rhythm to the ocean waves on the coast, which might be why many musicians claim Santa Barbara as their home. Before Katy Perry kissed a girl, perpetual laid-back dude Jack Johnson was selling out his shows at the Santa Barbara Bowl. Toad the Wet Sprocket came into being in 1986, and the members of the band, then students at San Marcos High School, worked diligently toward releasing their first album just three years later. Kenny Loggins has long been a staple of the area, lend-ing his name and concerts to charities and benefits, and the post-grunge band Dishwalla also hails from the city. Softcore ska-punkers Mad Caddies have been rollicking as a solid seven-piece band since they officially formed in Santa Barbara in 1995.

ⓘ The book *Island of the Blue Dolphins* was based on the true story of a woman stranded on San Nicolas Island, part of the Channel Islands. Juana Maria, also known as the "Lone Woman," was part of the Nicoleño tribe, and she lived on the island for eighteen years, from 1835 to 1853, all by her lonesome. Her tribe's population had dwindled to about twenty people by 1835, and they were removed from this remote island outpost stuck in the Pacific. How she was left on the island is a matter of dispute. What's not in dispute is that just seven weeks after she was "rescued" from the island and forced to Santa Barbara, she died. She's buried at Old Mission Santa Barbara, but no one knows where.

ⓘ At 6:48 a.m. on June 29, 1925, a thirty-square-block area of downtown was severely damaged. Sheffield Dam failed, plunging water into the area. Two acres of land west of the city sunk nearly a foot, Cabrillo Boulevard sustained cracks larger than twelve inches, and thirteen people died. Why? A magnitude 6.8 earthquake struck, that's why. Much of the cheap construction failed, and parts of commercial buildings on lower State Street, built on landfill, collapsed. Brick buildings and wood construction shattered, and some storefronts sheared off completely so that you could see directly inside the buildings.

ⓘ Architect Julia Morgan (of Hearst Castle fame) was in Santa Barbara when the earthquake hit. She had arrived early that morning holding blueprints for a meet-and-greet with the building committee. The quake was kind of a rude welcome. She spent that morning viewing the damage, noting which buildings had survived. Morgan became convinced of the need for reinforced concrete buildings, and thus rebar became a more common building practice.

ⓘ On February 23, 1942, the first attack on US soil since the War of 1812 occurred in little ol' Santa Barbara when a Japanese submarine shelled our coast. No damage was done, and the sub was never found, but many local Japanese residents were sent to internment camps.

ⓘ The NBC soap opera *Santa Barbara*, while not filmed here, was one of the most successful shows of its kind, even though it aired for just nine years. It was syndicated to more than forty countries and won twenty-four Daytime Emmy Awards. And, as a former actor, I had a small speaking part on one of the episodes. I was a bellman. The suit was mauve. I won't discuss it further.

ⓘ The Channel Islands are home to the oldest human remains in North America—more than 13,000 years old, to be precise—known as Arlington Springs Man (which actually sounds like a crappy band name).

ⓘ Along Highway 101 you'll see a bell atop a shepherd's hook with the words "Historic El Camino Real." These bells mark the original route of the King's Highway (the king of Spain, that is) that connected the Spanish missions. These paths were originally Indian footpaths, based on wild animal paths, and today they mark the basic trajectory of Highway 101, Highway 126, and Highway 1. The first commemorative bells along this six-hundred-mile route appeared in 1906. No, they don't ring.

*The King's Highway*

ⓘ Mr. Zog's Sex Wax was invented in 1972 in Goleta by chemist Nate Skinner and surfer Frederick Charles Herzog III. The brand remains a leading surfboard and snowboard wax and is produced from its Carpinteria headquarters.

## Arts and Galleries

**Architectural Foundation of Santa Barbara** (afsb.org, 229 E. Victoria St., 805/965-6307) Housed in an authentic Victorian residence, this gallery showcases the works of local and regional architects and artists. This is one of the few venues where local architects (and we have a bunch) can present not only images of their conceptual structural work but also their artistic work and cool renderings they have done. Not all architects can draw, mind you, but they certainly can sketch out ideas.

**Channing Peake Gallery** (www.sbac.ca.gov, 105 E. Anapamu St., 805/568-3990) That an art gallery exists on the first floor of the County Building is pretty nifty. That the rotating works, including paintings, photography, and even sculptures, are so good is even better. That it's free is best. It's located directly across from the county courthouse, so walk over, take in the art, and leave quickly. No one wants to stand around a county building for too long.

**Faulkner Gallery** (40 E. Anapamu St., 805/564-5608) This gallery is located inside the main branch of the public library, and most people walk right past it. The art rotates every few months, and there are two small side rooms with even more art, from plein air to still life. Everything is for sale, and these are mainly local artists. The art is less expensive than in traditional galleries and is worth checking out. There is some iffy stuff—you know, folks who truly believe they have a calling, but they don't—but a lot of talented people also show here. You don't need a library card to see it.

**Museum of Contemporary Art Santa Barbara** (www. mcasantabarbara.org, 653 Paseo Nuevo, 805/966-5373) This warehouse-sized space is devoted to, you know, contemporary art, be it visual, multimedia, performing arts, or just weird stuff that people make up and call art. The museum offers exhibitions which showcase the latest pieces by local, regional, national, and international artists and which often push the envelope for modern art. Since Santa Barbara is relatively devoid of wacky contemporary art exhibits, this is the place to stop when you're sick of seeing paintings of Spanish missions, coastline watercolors, or yet another eucalyptus tree.

**Santa Barbara Arts and Crafts Show** (sbaacs.com, Cabrillo Boulevard at Chase Palm Park, 805/897-1982) Every Sunday at the beach is the definitive arts and crafts show. More than one hundred local artists set up tables full of some very cool jewelry, wind chimes, vases, ceramics, and photography, as well as some bad art and other stuff, such as caricatures. This has been going on for thirty years (not continuously, just every Sunday like I said), and it's *free*. So stroll along the waterfront, people watch, art watch, and hang at the beach.

**Sullivan Goss** (sullivangoss.com, 11 E. Anapamu St., 805/730-1460) This is the most well-known art gallery in town. Owner Frank Goss knows his stuff and has a lot of it to share. The gallery has frequent exhibitions showcasing top talent from across the US, with an emphasis on the nineteenth through the twenty-first centuries. The main gallery is bright, open, and free. And yes, I have purchased paintings here.

## Festivals and Events

**Fiesta, a.k.a. Old Spanish Days** (oldspanishdays-fiesta. org) This five-day extravaganza held the first weekend of August is Santa Barbara's oldest festival. Started in 1924 to honor our Spanish and Mexican heritage, Fiesta has blossomed into the second largest equestrian parade in the US. I suppose that's a selling point, but after the first thirty horses go by, you kind of stop caring. Fiesta is a feast of Mexican food, cheap margaritas, and lots of dancing. There are three *mercados* (marketplaces) around town in which to partake of tortillas, burritos, tamales, tacos, and other Mexican food. There are also activities for the kids, such as climbing walls, mariachi bands, and rides.

During Fiesta, the Sunken Gardens at the Courthouse are transformed into a three-night free event stage, where singers and dancers from across the globe dance *folklorico*, flamenco, ballet, and hip-hop as singers belt out traditional Mexican songs, all under the beautiful evening skies of an August moon (please note: no teahouse). The courthouse, lit up and shining in her magnificence, is a beautiful venue for the concerts, and all you need to do is grab a blanket, chair, and picnic and you're set. Fiesta officially kicks off with La Fiesta Pequeña (the little fiesta) at the mission, with dances, local political figures (yawn), and a blessing by the mission fathers, and it includes tribal dances by native Chumash people. During the festivities, it's customary to buy hollowedout eggs that are painted and filled with confetti, crack them over the heads of friends

*There's lots of flamenco dancing during Fiesta.*

and loved ones, and shout, "Viva la Fiesta!" If you crack an egg over the head of someone you don't know, you run the risk of having an unpleasant Fiesta. This custom is nothing new and actually dates to the 1830s. Many locals flee town during Fiesta, as everything changes for the event: hotel room rates increase, parking is at a premium, and there are cover charges at bars and clubs and lines at restaurants. But it's still Fiesta, and it's only once a year.

**Harbor and Seafood Festival** (harborfestival.org, at the harbor, 805/897-1962, free) It's a no-brainer that Santa Barbara should have a seafood festival at the harbor because, you know, this is where the fishermen haul in their fish. Held each October, this one-day event brings out food vendors and artisans, and you can see cooking demonstrations, check out Coast Guard vessels, and even work remotely operated underwater vehicles (ROVs). You'll learn about the fish you consume, the water you play in, and the men and women who hit the ocean each day to bring in your seafood. It's all things celebrating the sea and our relationship with it. The **Santa Barbara Channel** is one of the nation's richest sources of seafood; lobsters, ridgeback shrimp, rock crabs, white sea bass, California halibut, yellowtail, salmon, swordfish, thresher sharks, spot prawns, and sea urchins all thrive here. About a hundred local fishermen catch about seven million pounds of seafood annually.

**I Madonnari Italian Street Painting Festival**
(imadonnarifestival.com, at the mission, free) When you were a kid, you might have defaced things—but if you got caught, you got in trouble. Here, people deface the mission and no one cares. Okay, that's not exactly true: people deface the parking lot at the mission. Held at the Old Mission Santa Barbara every Memorial Day weekend, the festival transforms the parking lot from icky asphalt to more than two hundred chalk paintings as artists—many local and some from across the globe—take chalk to blacktop

to create original drawings and beautiful reproductions of classic works of art. The mission lawn is crowded with food vendors, picnickers, and live bands, and you can watch the art in action. Just watch where you step.

**International Orchid Show** (sborchidshow.org, Earl Warren Showgrounds, 805/403-1533, $12) If you think orchids are just flowers, these people will yell at you. Orchid lovers are passionate about these plants, and for more than six decades about five thousand people annually have visited this festival, held each March. Thousands of unique, and in some cases bizarre, plants are displayed, and I do mean weird, funky, almost scary-looking plants. But there is a strange beauty to them. Experts are on hand to discuss orchids, how not to kill them, and how to purchase them (the orchids, not the experts). Santa Barbara has a mild, Mediterranean climate with temperate nights and soft, ocean breezes; orchids in Santa Barbara took root (ha-ha) at the turn of the century, when wealthy people came to escape harsh East Coast winters. Many built estates and commissioned world-class horticulturists and landscape architects to design elaborate gardens, and exotic orchids became way popular. And now we have a festival.

**Santa Barbara Beer Festival** (sbbeerfestival.com, at Elings Park) Yes, this is wine country, but that's why this stunningly popular beer festival sells out every October. A collection of thirty brewers from the West Coast and beyond gathers on the grassy fields at Elings Park under blue skies to celebrate the best brews. Get your pretzel necklace and wander about, listening to three different bands and sampling lots of food. If you tire of beer, there are some wines and even hard cider available. The cost runs about $50, and that's an amazing deal.

**Santa Barbara Foresters** (sbforesters.org) For some, baseball is a religion. If watching someone hit a home run, pick off second, or steal home is the pinnacle of your life, then know we have our very own baseball team. Games are played near the harbor at Pershing Park, and tickets are a measly $6, $1 for the kids. Take yourself out to the ball game if you're visiting during June or July. "If you show up, they will play."

**Solstice Parade**
(solsticeparade.com) This parade started in 1974 as an homage to local artists and as a pseudo-celebration of the summer solstice. Since those humble beginnings, the solstice parade has exploded into a free-for-all of color, costume, political incorrectness, dance, music, and just plain weirdo behavior—any excuse to get buzzed in public. Think of this as a West Coast Mardi Gras and you'll get the idea. Nearly a hundred thousand people

*Getting wild at the Solstice Parade*

cram the streets to celebrate the longest day of the year, and a thousand people volunteer in the effort. This isn't a well-organized parade, either; this is a fly-by-the-seat-of-your-pants, we-have-no-money-to-build-a-really-nice-float parade, so it ends up being fun precisely because it can't be sophisticated. The after-party at Alameda Park, with drumming circles, random dancing, food, vendors, live bands, and people wearing the bare minimum in the July sun is sometimes more fun than the parade itself.

## Health and Wellness

**Cat Therapy** (cattherapysb.com, 1213 State St., 805/560-1996) We're not being catty, but Cat Therapy is the only cat café between Los Angeles and San Francisco. Owner

Catalina (yes, that's her real name; yes, I understand the irony) is originally from Argentina but moved to Santa Barbara with a crazy idea to help adult cats get adopted. You book a reservation to hang out with the cats, make friends, play, let them sit on you, and read, and you can even have

*Cuddle with the kitties at Cat Therapy*

a party and book out the room. You can order food from a restaurant across the street and de-stress; however, no one will pet you—combing is for kitties. Some people are actively looking to adopt, while others visit because they just love animals. It's the purr-fect way to spend some time in Santa Barbara.

**Crimson Day Spa** (crimsondayspa.com, 31 Parker Way, 805/563-7546, by appointment) Facials, mani/pedis, body scrubs, acupuncture, aroma therapy, spa parties and waxing are just part of the offerings at Crimson. The spa uses plant-based products that are organic, EcoCert, and animal-cruelty free (yay!). The space is uncluttered, though it has nice touches of décor to suggest relaxation.

**Float Luxury Spa** (floatluxuryspa.com, 18 E. Canon Perdido St., 805/845-7777) Located downtown, this space is surprisingly large, sleek, and uncluttered. The spa offers the usual treatments, such as massages, facials, and the rest, but the atmosphere is better than any other spa in town. Out back is a beautiful tiled reflecting pool, which is a great spot to get lunch or take a deep breath. Upstairs the spa has a quiet space, a white room with chairs fronting a fireplace where you can sit and detox.

**Healing Circle Massage** (healingcirclemassage.com, 3040 State St., 805/680-1984, by appointment) This is where you go to get the kinks worked out of you. This isn't fluffy pampering while sipping cocktails and listening to flute music; this is deep tissue and trigger point work. Owner Dr. Kathy Gruver, a successful author on health and mind-body medicine, works on hardcore athletes and anyone with chronic pain, and she specializes in medical and therapeutic massage, meaning she'll rub you the right way. In addition to returning range of motion to stressed-out individuals (hopefully not you while on vacation), she also does prenatal massage, stress consulting, Reiki, and hypnotherapy. You're getting sleepy . . .

**The Spa at El Encanto** (belmond.com, 800 Alvarado Place, 805/845-5800) There is a luxury residential feel to the interiors of this spa; bathed in neutral colors, they are simple and clean without being pompous or ostentatious. All seven treatment rooms, which have fifteen-foot ceilings, emphasize natural lighting and minimalist décor to better focus your energy. All treatment rooms have individual temperature controls, and you can use your iPod to upload your own music. Seasonal body treatments range from lemon-basil in the summer to sage in autumn to peppermint in the winter, and all use sustainably grown herbs and include a salt body scrub and apricot-oil massage. Massages range from the traditional Swedish version to deep tissue and maternity, and the spa is kid-friendly, with mini mani/pedi treatments and thirty-minute massages for the young ones. The hair and nail salon offers multiple services, including shampoo and blow-dry services, updos, and of course traditional women's and men's haircuts and styling.

**The White Lotus Foundation** (whitelotus.org, 2500 San Marcos Pass Rd., 805/964-1944) If you're in the mood for a yoga retreat while you're here, this tucked-into-the-hillside retreat will stretch your horizons. Formed in 1983, White Lotus, located along Highway 154, has been dedicated to the principles of yoga ever since. Founder Ganga White says, "Everything's in flux right now, and we have an opportunity to change our lives. What's needed is a transformation in consciousness." Free will isn't free however, and throughout the year the foundation offers various retreats for a price including daily yoga classes, pranayama and meditation practices, vegetarian meals, hikes, music, dance, ceremonies, and guidance on diet and nutrition. Namaste.

## Museums

**Carriage and Western Art Museum** (carriagemuseum. org, 129 Castillo, 805/962-2353, free) Home to more than seventy horse-drawn carriages, most constructed between 1850 and 1911, this museum also has hand-tooled saddles, a few belonging to celebrities such as Clark Gable, Ronald Reagan, Jimmy Stewart, and Will Rogers. There's more tack than you'll know what to do with. Thinking this sounds dull? Neigh. Serious equestrian fans will be in heaven, and it's a reminder that there are no self-driving horses. It's a block from the beach, near the harbor, so you can easily fit it into your schedule. Many of these restored carriages are used during the Fiesta parade each August.

**The Karpeles Manuscript Library** (www.rain.org/~karpeles, 21 W. Anapamu St., 805/962-5322, free) Feeling bookish? This place might seem a tad dry as a sight to see, given that the name says it's all manuscripts. But manuscripts come in many forms, and the two-story building, which is predictably quiet inside, houses artifacts such as stone carvings—some of the earliest writings from 1,400 BC. There are also original documents, letters, and sections of diaries. While it may not take a long time to view the works represented, it is nonetheless impressive that the written word—this book, for example—continues to carry civilization forward.

**Reagan Ranch Center** (reaganranch.yaf.org, 217 State St., 805/957-1980, free) President Reagan had a history with Santa Barbara. His ranch, dubbed the Western White House, was perched atop the mountains between Santa Barbara and Solvang. It is still used today (not as the White House, because Reagan passed away in 2004—you know that, right?—and thus not open to the public. At the Reagan Ranch Center, however, you can get lots of info about those days, and many items from his ranch are on display, including his Jeep, desk, and chainsaw (maybe from when he tried to cut the deficit?). But the best part is a slab of the Berlin Wall . . . you know the line. It's an all-Reagan celebration, and you can't discount his legacy, not only for America but also for Santa Barbara.

**Santa Barbara Historical Museum** (www.sbhistorical.org, 136 E. De La Guerra, 805/966-1601, donation) The collection housed in this space is beautifully presented and includes an 1813 Peruvian mission bell, a three-foot-tall hand-painted wood carving of St. Barbara herself (I think she was taller in real life), and an exquisitely carved, intricate fifteen-foot Tong shrine from the days when Santa Barbara had a Chinatown. There are also garments from the presidio days, antique guns and swords, and an overall history of the area, from the Chumash through the Spanish, Mexican, and early American periods. Rotating exhibits feature anything from important local artists to designer Kem Weber's industrial work and furnishings representing his time teaching in town. The museum has a small gift store. A visit is nearly mandatory for anyone who desires an understanding of the multi-layered history of this area.

**Santa Barbara Maritime Museum** (sbmm.org, 113 Harbor Way, 805/962-8404, $8) Ahoy! Housed in an old naval building built during WWII—it has the dull, square look common to most government buildings—this two-story space opens up warmly and gives way to exhibits on surfing, shipwrecks (we've had lots of shipwrecks in the Channel), and a full-length tomol: a wood canoe the

Chumash used to paddle the twenty-six miles between the mainland and the islands—now there's a workout. Rotating exhibits with a common theme of the sea come and go like the tides (sorry). Anchor yourself here for an afternoon.

**Santa Barbara Museum of Natural History** (sbnature.org, 2559 Puesta del Sol, 805/682-4711, $10) The first thing you'll notice here is the skeleton of a real seventy-two-foot blue whale—and his name is Chad, thank you very much. Then you'll notice how small you are in comparison. Sitting just above and over Mission Creek, the collection of Spanish-themed buildings that make up this museum abuts a creek, and plenty of oak trees cover the property. The museum is small but spread out. There are exhibits on early Chumash life, including crafts; a small nature trail; a planetarium; sections devoted to vertebrate and invertebrate zoology, including a great bird section; a really cool display on gems and stones; and even a small fossil dig for kids out back. And no, they won't dig up real fossils, but there are bones planted in the dig sites so kids can feel like they are true archaeologists.

**Santa Barbara Museum of Art** (sbmuseart.org, 1130 State St., 805/963-4364, $10) Santa Barbara has a pretty darn impressive art museum for a city of its size. Two stories of rotating and permanent exhibits (don't worry, the floors stand still) will keep you busy. The museum showcases a large diversity of media, from print to photography, and has everything from Roman sculptures to abstract postmodern art. The collection of Asian art (including Japanese, Chinese, and Tibetan art) is one of the particular focuses. When the museum was founded in 1941, nineteen Chinese robes were donated, which started the Asian trend. Are there still nineteen cold Chinese folks somewhere in the world? Maybe. Today the Asian collection consists of more than 2,700 objects in a variety of media, spanning a period of 4,000 years (kon'nichiwa!).

## Nightlife

Many bars in Santa Barbara have small dance floors, but they are not dance clubs. One of the criticisms of the nightlife in town is that it seems amateurish compared to Los Angeles, New York, or any other major city. But that's exactly the point: Santa Barbara is not a major city, and the club experience here is very different, not trendy and flashy, though it may want to be.

**Arlington Theatre** (thearlingtontheatre.com, 1317 State St., 805/963-4408) This theater has the coolest interior of any theater you've ever seen. Used for film (the Santa Barbara Film Festival uses this as its main screen), lectures, dance, music, and most anything, it is classic Santa Barbara. The entrance is a long covered atrium with painted arches, a large fountain splashes out front, and there's a sweeping spire and red-tiled roof. Once you enter, the Spanish theme continues—the theater was designed to look like a courtyard. The walls themselves pop with balconies, red roofs, stairways, and porches; you are literally in the center of a Spanish village. It's the best place to see a movie or show, and the Santa Barbara architectural theme follows you inside.

**Astronomy On Tap** (lco.global/aot) With a tagline like "Science is better with beer," you know you're on the right trajectory. Monthly talks by astronomers and other people smarter than I am discuss black holes, death stars, dark matter—you know, all that stuff that's cool 'cause we don't get it. Held in a local bar, these are intimate, fun, and free (well, not the beer). This is a global thing, and locally it's sponsored by Las Cumbres Observatory, which builds super-duper high-end telescopes all over the globe. So check it out. Bazinga!

**Comedy Hideaway** (sbcomedy.com, 33 W. Victoria, 805/364-2999, $12) I just flew into Santa Barbara, and boy are my arms tired! Okay, so Santa Barbara isn't known as a funny place, but it finally does have a few comedy venues, featuring a few locals and lots of funny people from LA, including performers who have appeared on Showtime and Comedy Central. It's nice to find a place where you can laugh out loud for a reasonable price. Shows change weekly.

**Eos** (eoslounge.com, 500 Anacapa St., 805/564-2410) Santa Barbara's premier nicer nighttime destination is pretty much Eos. Its unique atmosphere blends the feel of a Mediterranean beach club with sleek furnishings and indoor and outdoor spaces. The crowd leans toward younger and well dressed, and because it's off State Street it doesn't get as many intoxicated walk-ins.

**The Hitchcock Cinema and Public House** (metrotheatres. com, 371 S. Hitchcock Way, 805/682-6512) We love the idea that Alfred Hitchcock drank beer—but that has nothing to do with this. Located on Hitchcock Way, this movie the-ater allows you to drink local wine or beer during the film. The theater doesn't show the current blockbusters; it's more of an arthouse place. But if merlot with a movie, or a saison with a screening, sounds like a great night out, here you go.

**Santa Barbara Bowl** (sbbowl.com, 1122 N. Milpas, 805/962-7411) With just over 4,500 seats, the bowl is a small, intimate venue that brings in big-name talent. It was built in the 1930s, and from its hillside location you can see the ocean and dance under the stars. There is no larger or more preeminent music venue in town, and for live music this is certainly the most beautiful. The stage setting is a little blocky—it would be nicer if the sandstone walls curved to better reflect its hillside location, but hey, this is still a killer spot to see a concert.

**SoHo Restaurant and Music Club** (sohosb.com, 1221 State St., 805/962-7776) SoHo is the premier mid-sized live music venue in town. Mondays are jazz nights, and other evenings offer everything from acoustic to funk.

SoHo has hosted its share of well-known acts, including David Crosby, Kenny Loggins, Rickie Lee Jones, Jimmy Cliff, the Mad Caddies, Acoustic Alchemy, and others. It has a second-floor outdoor patio, which is a prime spring and summer location to enjoy the music under a canopy of stars. The restaurant portion is hit and miss—but you come here to hear music, not eat.

**Velvet Jones** (velvet-jones.com, 423 State St., 805/965-8676) This club offers live music seven nights a week, and many of the musicians are up-and-comers from Los Angeles. The space isn't going for looks, but it does go for hard rock, grunge, hip-hop—anything other than middle-of-the-road music. If you remember who Karen Carpenter was, this may not be the place for you. It has a small kitchen serving hot dogs and pizza, but that's it. A small interior balcony and medium-sized dance floor give you space so you're not crammed in, and a small gated front patio lets you cool down before you heat up again.

## Outdoor Activities

### AIR

**Fly Above All Paragliding** (flyaboveall.com, 2550 Cliff Dr., 805/965-3733) This outfit offers a beginning two-flight deal (tandem with an instructor) at Elings Park for $100. The flights are pretty short but really fun, and this is a great starting point if you've never done it. It offers full classes, as well. This isn't hang gliding; this is paragliding, where you're harnessed into the chute and use a running start to get into a vertical position. Then it's all downhill from there . . . so to speak.

### EARTH
### *Bike*

Santa Barbara is a bike-friendly place, but we don't pedal that a lot. From flat beachfront rides to challenging uphill mountain paths to meandering roads through wine country, there is something for every level of rider, even those in a stroller. Regardless of your skill level, when you pass another cyclist, always call out "on your left" to alert riders ahead of you to move over. Contact SmartRide at info@trafficsolutions.info or 805/963-SAVE to obtain a copy of the Santa Barbara County bike map ($2.95) in either English or Spanish; it shows class levels for the entire county, different routes, rules of the road, and other important info. SmartRide also has free apps to download.

**Coast Route** This bike path for the most part hugs the coast near the waterfront, then climbs into a residential area and drops you down near Arroyo Burro Beach. From there the road climbs into Hope Ranch, a beautiful and well-to-do section of Santa Barbara with a stunning concentration of mature trees. Eventually you hit the Atascadero Bike Path, which shuttles you through low marshlands before arriving at UCSB. You can continue on from there and hook up with the Foothill Route to make a wide loop, but that's a taxing ride.

**Foothill Route** Also known as Highway 192, also known as Cathedral Oaks, this route alternates from narrow stretches of road around Mission Canyon to flat, wide streets near Winchester Canyon by the beach. It's very popular because of its many hills, and you can ride from the beach in Goleta all the way into Ojai in Ventura County. There is a lot of traffic around the Mission Canyon area, and as the road climbs it twists and turns, so cyclists need to be on the lookout for cars coming around blind curves. Between Mission Canyon and Goleta, the road widens and takes you past avocado orchards and citrus ranches until it leads into Winchester Canyon by the water.

**Hope Ranch** Though they don't want you to cycle in their neck of the woods, this wealthy enclave of hills and equestrian paths is stunningly beautiful. There are no maps, and this residential area is quiet and peaceful, with plenty of hills and curves. The best place to start is to park on Modoc Road near the entrance to the bike bath, near Lyric Lane.

**Waterfront Course** This is the most common bike route; all flat and pretty, it runs from the Andree Clark Bird Refuge, past the zoo, and beyond City College up on the mesa. It's easy and scenic and is ideal for guests without much stamina. You can rent bikes, including tandem bikes and four-person surreys, along Cabrillo Boulevard. You can also rollerblade, skateboard, walk, skip, meander, and lounge on this path.

### *Channel Islands National Park*

The five Channel Islands are Santa Barbara's backyard. (Your backyard might be smaller.) Four border the Central Coast within eye shot: Anacapa, Santa Cruz, Santa Rosa, and San Miguel. Santa Barbara and San Nicolas (San Nicolas is not part of the park) are small and not visible from the coast; they are the least visited because there's not much there and it takes a long time to get out to them. And they're lonely.

For more than thirty years, these islands have been federally protected. Long before they were tourist spots, they were ranch lands. Santa Cruz Island in particular was prime grazing land for cattle and sheep in the 1800s, without the worry of predators like those on the mainland (I mean animals, not people). Santa Cruz was also home to a winery, and the decaying remnants are still standing. And even longer before that the Chumash people lived on the islands—as long as 13,000 years ago. They were mainly fish eaters, and the bulk of what they left behind were known as "middens," trash heaps full of bones, seashells, and whatever other trash they threw away. Now historians sift through the minutia of their garbage. Not how I like to spend my time.

The peculiar thing is that, although the islands are relatively close to the mainland, a preponderance of locals have never visited their own backyard. Inexpensive day trips allow you to explore, hike, kayak, snorkel, camp, and scuba dive at the islands. Multi-day trips allow for camping in the interiors and for visiting several islands. To sail there can take four hours, and motorboats make it even faster, and yet people don't explore. Perhaps it's because the islands look so far away. Yet Anacapa is only twelve miles from Ventura Harbor. Anacapa, Santa Cruz, and to a lesser degree Santa Rosa can be done as day trips, though only Santa Cruz and Anacapa trips are available year-round. I have visited Santa Cruz, Anacapa, and Santa Rosa and sailed to them many times, and there is always the wonderful feeling that these islands are some of the last vestiges of pristine and unadulterated life on the West Coast. They retain a purity we all long for and at least a small glimpse into how life was before shopping malls and cellphone towers.

**Channel Islands Visitor Center** (nps.gov/chis, 1901 Spinnaker Dr., Ventura, 805/658-5730) At the visitor center, located in Ventura rather than Santa Barbara, there are topographical maps of five of the islands, as well as cool 3-D maps you can touch to get a better feel for the islands. The fourth-floor observation tower has great views to Ventura Harbor and the islands. There are books and other info about the islands, and the rangers can answer your questions. A pygmy mammoth skeleton is on display, the original of which is at the Santa Barbara Natural History Museum. There's also a touch tank with garibaldi (the California state fish), lobster (no butter included), starfish, and other creatures. The park rangers have tidepool talks at 11 a.m. and 3 p.m., with a fish feeding at 3 p.m. that is great for kids. About 200,000 visitors go to the islands each year—so when you come to the Central Coast, seriously consider taking a day and getting out there.

**Anacapa Island** This island is best known for Arch Rock, a geologic formation of the islands that is, you know, an arched rock. Though you can't access Arch Rock on foot (unless you've mastered walking on water), you can sail by it or kayak underneath it. This volcanic formation has become an indelible landmark of the island. The entrance to Anacapa is predictably named Landing Cove, a small harbor where boats anchor. The harbor is small, and the waters can get rough. You take a Zodiac to a metal ladder, and up you go to the island. There are 154 steps to the top of the island. There are sheer cliffs almost all the way around Anacapa. On top the vegetation is sparse and low, and there are few trees. From the top you can clearly see the "spine" of the island, which curves and bends toward Santa Cruz Island. It is a stunning display of volcanic formations, with multiple smaller islands forming a chain that extends for five miles. Anacapa also has about 130 sea caves and is home to the largest brown pelican rookery in the US. You'll discover that fact after you land, as the stench is obvious in certain spots. An old lighthouse hugs the far end, making for cool photo ops. Travel time is about an hour each way, and you're very likely to see dolphins on the way.

*Arch Rock at Anacapa Island*

**Santa Cruz Island** This is the largest of the islands, some twenty-two miles long. There are more old buildings on this island than on the others, and there is a day camp near Scorpion Bay where you can pitch a tent (or pitch a fit if you get seasick), store your food in metal lockers, and set out to explore on foot. There are trees here, and old, dried-out creek beds—often barren depending on the winter rains—that speak of what was once grassland. This used to be farmland—hard to believe, but true. Being so far removed from the mainland, the cattle operations dwindled out in the 1920s because it was discovered that cows couldn't swim. Actually, ranching started here because there were no natural predators, but it got expensive. The elusive and nimble Channel Islands fox lives here, and frankly my cat is bigger than this guy. There are ravens, too. It's also the only place in the world to see the island scrub jay—probably not a huge selling point for most people. This is by far the most popular island to visit; it most closely resembles the mainland, and frankly it is the most hospitable. Travel time is an hour each way. Once there you offload onto a short pier directly to shore, though shore landings from a skiff are possible depending on conditions. Santa Cruz is a vast piece of land, and it's best to visit the center of the island if possible. There the vegetation is thick, dense, and nearly *Jurassic Park*-like in its appearance. You half expect to find some strange prehistoric animal on this island calmly eating a tree. The best way to explore is by kayak or boat to really get a feel for the beauty of the rock formations, the multi-colored strata of the rock, and the numerous coves and tiny beaches that are still relatively unused. Seals and sea lions make their homes in some of these coves, and the craggy rocks are home to oystercatchers, eagles, pelicans, and plenty of other animals that crave the security and tranquility of these pockets of land. Painted Cave is here; it is the longest sea cave and one you can kayak into.

**Santa Rosa Island** This island is a bit more forlorn than Santa Cruz, with low, flat grass and some trees in the old water ravines. Aside from that, there is minimal shade. Again, the steep cliffs prohibit landing just anywhere. There are some beautiful white sand beaches, though, and coastal lagoons and other places you need to seek out that seem virtually untouched, as if no one has walked these shores before. The vistas from the top of some of the plateaus are beautiful, with views to neighboring Santa Cruz Island and the California coastline in the distance. Travel time is about three hours each way by boat, and you'll need to climb a twenty-foot steel rung ladder to reach the island's flat land.

**San Miguel Island** You can visit this island via a concession tour for only part of the year. It is a remote and desolate place, with fierce winds that can, at times, prohibit land-ing here. But the stark beauty is enchanting to some, and there are more species of birds, plants, and animals here than on the other islands. Stories abound that Juan Rodrí-guez Cabrillo, the first Westerner to set eyes on the West Coast, in 1542, died and was buried here. Yes, there is a small memorial to him in Cuyler Harbor, a white cross planted firmly in the hard earth. Yes, it's also true that when Cabrillo landed at the islands (not in Santa Barbara as many believe; he never touched the mainland) he became sick and died. But specific dates and his burial place are a matter of conjecture. Some say his crew buried him at San Miguel, and some say they took his body to Catalina Island off the coast near Long Beach—ah, conspiracy theories abound. Regardless of historical hypotheses, there is no definitive proof of exactly where Cabrillo's bones remain. The island, used for cattle and sheep grazing until just after World War II, then became a bombing range for the mili-tary to practice on—yikes. Travel time is about four hours each way from Santa Barbara. Usually a skiff will run you to shore, depending on the weather conditions, which can be hit and miss.

**Santa Barbara Island** This island is little more than a small rock in the lonely Pacific and is virtually impossible to see from the mainland. There are campsites on these 644 acres, but if you stayed you'd have to wonder exactly why you were here. Shut off, secluded, and lonely, it's a rare stop for most people, in spite of the occasional lush vegetation that grows here. Travel time is just over three hours; once there, you will have to not only climb a steel rung ladder from a skiff but also laboriously trudge up a quarter-mile set of steps to reach the top. Once there, you won't find any shelter, but you will be on one of the least visited islands, and it is a very cool feeling to know that few people have walked this land before you.

### Picnics: Best Tucked-Away Spots

In Santa Barbara it's almost always time for a picnic. But finding the best and coolest picnic spots may be harder than you think. Everyone knows the obvious choices: Leadbetter Beach with its numerous tables, Tucker's Grove Park with its family amenities, Shoreline Park, and such. So I scoured the beaches, mountains, and parks to find five lesser-known but still classic Santa Barbara picnic places that are more secluded and offer diverse views. Pack your picnic basket and discover some alfresco undercover gems of Santa Barbara.

**Franceschi Park** For the absolute best views of the city, this under-the-radar park located on the Riviera has unsurpassed vistas to downtown, the harbor, the ocean, and the islands and is flanked by large eucalyptus trees. Part botanical garden, part city park, it is fairly secluded and quiet. It is set in a residential area, and there is no food available nearby. There are a few picnic tables and benches facing the ocean, and also the dilapidated but wonderfully odd Franceschi House with its unusual embellishments (the house is not open to the public). The park is open sunrise to sunset; there is limited parking and a restroom on site.

**Andree Clark Bird Refuge** Set in a riparian woodland, the refuge has three small wooden platforms with benches on them jutting out over the water, the last one being over a small bridge near the Santa Barbara Zoo. These platforms are accessed by a flat path that circumscribes part of the lake. You can sit directly above the water, with the cool breezes from East Beach washing over you, and you can have a modicum of privacy and quiet, although the plat-forms are not shaded. As the water laps at your feet, you'll probably see diverse birds, including the occasional white pelican. The refuge is located close to Coast Village Road in Montecito, and food and restrooms are a short drive away.

**Elings Park** Though it's a popular spot for weddings, Cedric Grove atop Elings Park has easy car access, not to mention serene views back toward the city. There are restrooms nearby, plenty of picnic tables, and a circular lawn surrounded by large, mature oak trees. There is no food available here, and there is a charge for parking on weekends, though weekday parking is free. Take the road all the way to the top and turn left on George Bliss Road. The Wells Fargo Amphitheater offers the best views of the city, not to mention plenty of graded seating. Benches flank both sides of the hill, one side looking toward the city and the other with views toward the park and out to the ocean.

**Lookout Park** Located in Summerland, right off High-way 101, Lookout Park is a small, grassy bluff above the beach. There are benches, picnic tables, and barbecue stands throughout the narrow park, with plenty of parking available. The grass, however, is very uneven, so watch your step. There is also a children's play area with swings and slides, a volleyball net on a sandy court, restrooms,

*A private picnic at the Bird Refuge*

horseshoes, and beach access. Dogs are allowed but must
be kept on a leash. This is an ideal spot for family or large
group picnics. Lillie Avenue is just two blocks away should
you need to purchase food.

**Sand Spit** Located at the termination of the breakwater
at the harbor, Sand Spit has a few whale-tail benches on
which to sit and watch Santa Barbara splayed out in front
of you. You can also bring your own chairs and head across
a short rock outcropping directly to the sand itself. To the
right is Sterns Wharf, to the left are the boats moored in
the harbor, in front of you is the city, and behind you is
the majestic Pacific; it's the best of all worlds. Take it all in:
feel the gentle ocean breezes and hear the sea lions on the
green buoy markers, but bring a hat as there is no shade.
Restrooms, food, and parking are all available at the main
buildings at the harbor.

## Golf

**Glen Annie Golf Club** (glenanniegolf.com, 405 Glen Annie
Rd., Goleta, 805/968-6400) Part of what makes this par-
seventy-two course so beautiful is that it's tucked into the
mountains facing the ocean. Well, to be fair, the city of
Goleta is between the course and the ocean, but you can

still see it! In conjunction with Audubon International, this course is one of six golf courses in California that support an Environmental Enhancement Program, which means the course doubles as a wildlife refuge for migratory birds (insert your own birdie joke here). Three different habitats provide homes to numerous wild animals, so if you go looking for that lost ball, you won't be alone.

**Rancho San Marcos** (rsm1804.com, 4600 Highway 154, 805/683-6334) This course was built on the site of the historic Rancho San Marcos, from 1804. Designed by Robert Trent Jones, Jr., the course gracefully straddles the natural topography, meandering among ancient oaks and preserved traces of nineteenth-century adobe structures. The eighteen-hole, par-seventy course sits off the San Marcos Pass, just fifteen miles from Santa Barbara and Solvang. It ain't cheap to play this course, with its oak-studded fairways and proximity to the mountain range, but it is less crowded.

**Sandpiper Golf Course** (sandpipergolf.com, 7925 Hollister Ave., 805/968-1541) This is the "poor man's Pebble Beach," which is a little rude, but true. This is one of the most beautiful courses in town. Sandpiper, a par seventy-one, provides killer views from the bluffs above the ocean and expert-level play. It's the only actual oceanfront course between Los Angeles and Monterey. The facilities are a little old, but the course is view-centric, assuming you care more about views than your scorecard.

### Hikes

Santa Barbara presents a diverse topography for hikes, from ocean bluffs to front country to the rugged back country. These four hikes give you assorted scenic vistas, a moderate workout, and great photo ops. A note on hiking in Santa Barbara, and all along the Central Coast: Yes, we have poison oak, so always be cautious when going off trail. It can't kill you, though rest assured—as a native Californian and having had my share of it—it ain't fun.

A note about park rangers: All across the county, rangers are cracking down on those who don't obey the rules—dogs on a leash, no biking, etc. So follow the rules of each place, because you don't want to get cited for something silly. OK? Always bring water, a hat, a cellphone, and sunscreen when you hike. My small pack also includes a knife, and nuts for protein, just in case. So get packed and get going! Check out santabarbarahikes.com, which is way more comprehensive than we can be here. Author Robert Stone has published a series of hiking books, including *Day Hikes Around Santa Barbara*, and I can't recommend them enough; they are packed with very detailed info!

## What to Do If You See a Scary Animal on a Hike

Yes, our foothills have bobcats, coyotes, snakes, tarantulas, and more. I've seen them all.

**1st Rule:** Don't bother them. Mind your business and they will mind theirs.

**2nd Rule:** Don't freak out. They are animals: they don't have guns or knives, they rarely carry nunchucks, and they will not hurt you.

**3rd Rule:** You are a guest. This is their home, not yours, so respect where you are. Don't make sudden noises, flail your arms about, or do anything hyper. Be calm and carry on.

**Arroyo Hondo Preserve** (sblandtrust.org) This is eight hundred acres of pure California. There are six miles of trails, from easy strolls through flat meadows to the difficult Outlaw Trail, so named because of the narrow canyon and its streamlined views to the road; Hondo was a refuge for outlaws in the late 1800s. The Outlaw Trail takes you from

34

the mouth of the canyon far up into the mountain, with killer views (funny). The trail is really two parts, starting with a low-key stroll through the Hollister meadow, which stops at a small grass clearing with a wooden picnic table placed strategically so you can rest and enjoy the ocean views. If this easy "hike" seems taxing, don't bother with the rest of the trail. From here it ascends sharply into the mountains, and you leave behind the lush meadow by the stream. As you ascend, the vegetation becomes sparser and lower to the ground, the heat becomes more pronounced, and the land more unforgiving. Heading up the Outlaw Trail, you pass through successive layers of rock formations, some estimated to be about forty million years old. At the top are sweeping views and a cool malformed sandstone outcropping that looks more like swiss cheese, with holes and tunnels permeating its core. You can stand up there and feel like you own the whole world. The views to the Pacific and the Channel Islands are unsurpassed. It's just you and the random hawks and turkey vultures that silently soar above you. To your left is the Tajiguas Landfill (which one local paper described as the "prettiest and most expensive landfill" in the tri-counties), and the peculiar juxtaposition of the two canyons—one a nature preserve and one a garbage dump—is amusing, if not a little sad. But that's why Arroyo Hondo is preserved: it won't end up being a dumping ground for our insatiable need to waste things. Hondo is open the first and third weekends of each month. There are free docent-led hikes the first Saturday and third Sunday of every month at 10 a.m. There's no cost to visit, but donations are accepted. Advance reservations are required (do this online) as a way of knowing who comes out, in part because the gates get locked and you don't want to be stuck here. From Santa Barbara, go north on Highway 101; Arroyo Hondo is four miles past Refugio State Beach. Look for the blue Caltrans call boxes spaced one mile apart on the righthand side of the highway. The

Arroyo Hondo entrance is located immediately after call box 101-412.

**Lizard's Mouth** (West Camino Cielo Rd.) For a completely different experience, head to Lizard's Mouth, so named for the unusual sandstone outcroppings—not for giant man-eating lizards. On the south-facing slopes of the mountain, with panoramic views of all of Santa Barbara and the Channel Islands (and quite possibly China . . . well, maybe not), this is a sea of wondrous boulders—curvilinear smooth sandstone, windswept and eerie, that seems to have been sculpted by hand. Take Highway 154 up from Santa Barbara seven miles to West Camino Cielo and turn left. Follow the road four miles to the Winchester Gun Club entrance. Turn around here. On your righthand side, about a hundred yards back down the road, you'll see a graffiti-sprayed brown wooden sign, about twenty feet off the road. There are no real paths here; you just wander in between large boulders and on top of sandstone flats. Some boulders you can walk underneath, and you swear they might collapse on you. It almost looks like a movie set; Lizard's Mouth has an otherworldly moonscape feel. It's easy to get lost, so keep an eye on where you came from. Small trails head out to, and in between, the rocks, some with small crevices and near cave-like entrances. It's pretty much rock hopping out here. It's a little disconcerting to hear the gunfire from the Winchester Gun Club up the road at first, but you're perfectly safe. Weekdays are better as it's less crowded.

**Rattlesnake Canyon** This is one of the more popular hikes and is fairly easy, and, no, you won't come across any rattlesnakes. It was named for its serpentine shape, not for giant man-eating rattlesnakes. This is a well-marked trail and is less than four miles in total. You'll pass by pools and streams and eventually come out the top of a small hill with panoramic views to the ocean and the Channel

Islands. From Los Canelos Road near the Santa Barbara Botanic Garden, it's just over one mile to the second stone bridge, where there is ample parking on the road pullouts. Starting on the trail it feels like you've been deceived; it's hot and dry and uninteresting. After ten minutes on the trail there's a short incline where you encounter two oak trees—go left (going right is a short trail, nothing exciting). You soon hook up with the creek in a wooded area and then cross the creek and head up into sheer diversity. You'll likely see grey squirrels and wild bunnies (not mean, just wild). It will take you forty minutes at a moderate pace to reach Tin Can Meadow, which is a great turnaround point. There's a flat rock there where you can sit for a while, surrounded by tall grass, and absorb the beauty before heading back. There is a terrific variety of stuff here, including multiple stream crossings, wooded areas, narrow open trails, moss-covered boulders, pine and oak trees, low scrub, and thick trees. With an elevation gain of nine hundred feet, it's a decent workout.

**San Marcos Foothills Preserve** (sanmarcosfoothills.com) So this is my backyard. Well, not literally, but I live nearby and am here most days (so if you see me, say hi). As the name suggests, this is a nature preserve, so bring your dog, but it must stay on a leash, and you too must stay on the wide paths. As you ascend the mild hills, you're treated to glorious views of the islands and the Pacific. This is one of the most underused nature areas (which suits me just fine), but it is ripe with its own beauty. You'll nearly always see hawks, quail, rabbits, and even road runners. From Foothill Road near the Highway 154 entrance, head north up Via Chaparral. When you see the bridge on your right (called the "bridge to nowhere," which is untrue 'cause it does go somewhere) turn right, then left, and then the road ends and the trail begins. Head straight up for panoramic views, or take the trail to your right to wind down into the canyon. Either way, this is easy to get to, easy to hike, and very pretty in its Old School California way.

### Labyrinths

Often overlooked, labyrinths can be an important respite in the midst of a busy day or vacation. There are several scattered around town, but these two provide everything you need: namely, you can walk in circles and no one will say anything to you about it. The easily accessible **Trinity Episcopal Church** (trinitySB.org, 1500 State St., 805/965-7419) on State and Micheltorena will challenge your concentration because it's on a major, noisy street. The gothic stone church is the perfect backdrop for this poured-in-place concrete labyrinth. If it freaks you out to have people watch you walking in circles, try the labyrinth at **UCSB** (wellness.ucsb.edu), which is not nearly as accessible. If anyone is watching you, that would just be creepy because it's not near anything— but that's what makes it cool. River stones on a dirt substrate path mark the course. You'll hear the rumbling of waves nearby and see serene views of the Channel Islands; this labyrinth is located on a bluff just up from the lagoon. It's

*The labyrinth at UCSB*

free, but it will take a walk to get there, and you'll need to pay for parking while on campus.

## Parks

**Alice Keck Park Memorial Gardens** (1500 Santa Barbara St.) These gardens are named for Alice Keck Park—see, that's her name, and this is not really a park but a garden. Are we clear on that? Once the site of a private residence turned hotel called the El Mirasol, Alice K. Park donated the plot of land, 4.6 acres, to the city to make a garden in perpetuity (meaning forever unless lawyers get involved). Now it's an awesome spot with a large grassy area, a turtle and koi pond, a gazebo, and wandering dirt paths with lots of cool plants—and some pretty handsome views to the mountains. Well planned out and calming, it's a great little spot in the middle of the city.

**Chase Palm Park** (236 E. Cabrillo Blvd.) This park has a European sensibility: a long, winding park with diverse set-tings and themes. There is the carousel, the duck pond, a grassy area where free concerts occur during the summer, and the shipwreck playground—looking less like a ship-wreck and more like an actual playground. It's across the street from the beach and can be less crowded than the grassy area that fronts the beach.

**Elings Park** (elingspark.org, 1298 Las Positas Rd., 805/969-5611) This former landfill is now a 230-acre park that offers everything from a BMX course and radio-controlled car racing to paragliding, a soccer and rugby field, wedding venues, hiking trails, picnic areas, and perfect views of the harbor, mountains, and ocean. This is a wonderful gem of a spot. Just the hiking alone on the moderate hills will take you to some great vistas. There is paid parking on week-ends, but it's free during the week.

**Franceschi Park** (1510 Mission Ridge Rd.) This is actually an old, dilapidated estate. Sounds fun, right? This is the former residence of Italian horticulturist Francesco Franceschi, who planted mini parks all along the Riviera; he acclimatized plants and introduced a number of tropical plant species into Santa Barbara. The house is closed to the public, but the grounds of this eighteen-acre park are open and free. This little-known spot has some of the best views of the city, harbor, and coastline, especially at sunset. There's a small parking lot and a few picnic tables, and the scent of eucalyptus permeates the air. Rarely visited, it's a cool spot perched in the hills.

**Rocky Nook Park** (610 Mission Canyon Rd.) Not Rocky Balboa, but Rocky Nook, this park is mildly rocky, and the nook refers to something we don't know from when the original owners bought this land in 1882. It's across from Old Mission Santa Barbara, and Mission Creek runs through it. Simple trails crisscross the rustic, non-grassy park, and it's a wonderful respite or place for a picnic. BBQ stands and a children's playground are all shaded by beautiful old oaks. It's easy to imagine the Chumash using the stream here, which they did, as there is a rustic beauty to this place.

**Santa Barbara Botanic Garden** (sbbg.org, 1212 Mission Canyon Rd., 805/682-4726, $12) The garden is seventy-eight acres of wilderness founded in 1926. Redwoods grow along shaded creeks, old oaks fan out everywhere, and there's a small Japanese tea house. The mission of the garden (that will be funny in a second) is to conduct horticultural research and to educate the public. By 1936 the emphasis was plants native to the state of California, northwestern Baja California, and southwestern Oregon, which are part of the California Floristic Province. A rich history is represented here, including part of the original mission aqueduct (see, that was funny) that fed the Old Mission Santa Barbara with clean water. Today there are six miles of walking trails and more than a thousand species of plants to check out. The library contains fifteen thousand volumes of works related to the disciplines of botany and horticulture, ironically written on paper made from trees.

## Run/Walk

There are many more races than those listed here, but these are some of the best, keeping you within sight of the Pacific Ocean.

**Nite Moves** (runsantabarbara.com) This 5K (3.1 miles, for our metrically challenged friends) is held each Wednesday from May to September along the coast. Anyone can race for a small fee, and you can add the open-water swim if you like. There's food, music, and awards, all starting at Leadbetter Beach as the sun begins to set. It's not flat, but it's also not difficult. With so many people out, you probably won't be the slowest in your age group.

**Pier to Peak** (runsantabarbara.com) This 13.1-mile (that's a half-marathon, folks) race each September starts at Stearns Wharf at sea level and takes you on a point-to-point course up nearly four thousand feet to La Cumbre Peak. Yes, you see much of Santa Barbara, the ocean, the mountains, and the mission, but you may not care. It's a tough race because it's basically all uphill, but it's extraordinarily satisfying.

**Franceschi Steps** (1400 block of Dover Rd.) Italian dude Francesco Franceschi, mentioned above, not only built a garden on the slanted hills of the Riviera but also cut into the hillside steps leading to his estate. The county then expanded on these steps, and now there is a weird series of steps perfect for a workout above Santa Barbara. Some are stone, some are paved, some are cut through egress sections of yards, and others fan out across the hills. It's easy to get lost, but it's so cool not only as a workout but also for the views. If you start at Dover Road (and you can start most anywhere) you'll end up near the entrance to Franceschi Park. It is weird, wild, un-mapped, and almost unknown. Step into an alternative workout.

**More Mesa** This is, hands down, the single best spot to run. Three hundred undeveloped bluff-top acres with loads of trails give you views to the ocean and islands and unfettered views to the mountains. It's also relatively isolated. Yes, there are a few walkers, other runners, and occasional off-road cyclists, and once—true story—I saw a woman running with her pony! The bluff-top trail inches its way to the cliffs, in some cases within a foot or two. A misstep and you'll plummet 150 feet to the surf below. This is my favorite spot to run, cycle, and power walk. In addition to the views, there is beach access down an old stair system built into the cliff. Chances are you'll see dolphins (in the ocean, not on the trails), a variety of birds, the occasional whale, maybe a fox, skunks, and snakes. More Mesa is accessed off Patterson Avenue in Goleta going south. Patterson turns into Shoreline Road and makes a right curve into Orchid. The trail leading to More Mesa will be on your left. Park at the bottom of the hill and walk up.

**The Waterfront** (Cabrillo Boulevard) This is where most tourists run and cycle. But because you bought this book you're not "most tourists." The concrete path is perfectly fine for a three- to four-mile out and back, running the length of the ocean and past the zoo toward the bird refuge. It can get crowded in the late mornings (as sleepyheads emerge to start their days) and in the afternoons. It's also important to watch out for rollerbladers, cyclists, and those who rent four-wheel surreys, as the steering mechanism isn't the greatest. But as you run by the ocean, with towering palm trees swaying gently in the breeze, you can't help thinking you're in paradise. There are restrooms and drinking fountains along the way.

**Mountain Drive** This is an asphalt road with gentle slopes and turns; because it's cut into the mountains, you get great views. Mountain Drive is also a long road, and you can run it for a long time. There are no services, however, as this is a residential area. If you park near the Sheffield Dam (West Mountain and Mission Ridge) and head north to Mountain Drive, turn right and begin. Sunday mornings are best as the traffic is the lightest. After about two miles you'll see on your right a mailbox in the shape of a chubby cyclist, whose rear end is where the mail goes (how's that for special delivery?). As many have done before, slap his butt and either head back or continue on.

**Hope Ranch** This wealthy enclave of hills and equestrian paths is stunningly beautiful. Follow the bridle paths most anywhere, past the small lake, under a canopy of oak trees, and out to the bluffs overlooking the ocean. There are no maps, and this residential area is quiet and peaceful. The best place to start is to park on Modoc Road near the entrance to the bike bath, near Lyric Lane.

## FIRE

**Fourth of July Fireworks** (the waterfront, 9 p.m. on, you know, July 4) Santa Barbara is obviously a small town, but the fireworks show, shot from a barge in the harbor and running about twenty minutes, is for all intents and purposes a really, really good show. If you're in town, do make a point of checking it out. You can watch from a distance on the hills, but it's best to be down by the waterfront with all the people, close to the action. Even better is to get on someone's boat in the harbor and just get happy.

## WATER
### Beaches

Beaches in Santa Barbara are generally long and flat. At low tide you can clearly see the rocks hidden under the waves—great for tide-pooling. Water temperatures in the summer are about sixty-one to sixty-two degrees, fifty-six to fifty-eight in winter. Because of several creeks running into the ocean and the inability to keep the creeks clean from people throwing their garbage into them, there are occasional closures for some beaches after heavy storms—they post signs, so please don't ignore them. Though there are lifeguards during peak summer hours, they disappear once the crowds do.

**Leadbetter Beach** (Shoreline Drive and Loma Alta) Leadbetter is a large city beach and park adjacent to the Santa Barbara Harbor. Many catamaran sailors and wind surfers use this beach to launch from, and you'll see occasional surfers riding tiny waves. The beach has a grassy picnic and barbecue site you can reserve, and where I was married. Think of me if you go here, in my younger, lighter, more fit days of yore. Home to many races and sporting events, the beach can get packed during a festivity. There are restrooms, a small restaurant, and outdoor showers. Directly across the street is Santa Barbara City College. If you enter the stadium and walk up the many steps, you'll get some terrific views of the harbor, plus you'll get a mini-workout.

**Arroyo Burro Beach** (at Cliff Drive and Las Positas) Known locally as Hendry's, this beach at the mouth of Arroyo Burro Creek is dog friendly. With a restaurant on site (decent food, but pricey) and a small grassy area for picnics, it's popular with locals and far removed from the downtown beaches, though it can still become very crowded on summer days. Summer sunsets at low tide are awesome. There are restrooms and outdoor showers. It's flanked by large cliffs, of which the Douglas Family Preserve (known locally as the Wilcox Property) is a favorite. A seventy-acre eucalyptus-studded (also dog-friendly) preserve, the blufftop location means few tourists even know about it. The parcel was planned for a housing development until actor Michael Douglas gave a substantial gift (I think it was cash, not his Oscar. Wait, did he win an Oscar?), enabling the parcel to remain un-built (and now ruled by dogs). He then named it after his father, actor Kirk Douglas.

**Goleta Beach** (5986 Sandspit Rd.) Located at the base of the UCSB campus, this beach is popular because of the picnic tables, BBQ pits, horseshoes, fishing, its long pier, and easy access to the water for kayakers and swimmers. The grassy area is partially shaded by trees, and there's also a small jungle gym for the kids. The pier is popular for fishing, and you can also launch small boats from here. It's less touristy than other beaches, and you can follow the bluffs into UCSB on a trail all the way to and around the lagoon. There's also a restaurant on site.

**El Capitán State Beach** (parks.ca.gov, 805/968-1033) Located seventeen miles west of Santa Barbara, El Cap (that's what we locals call it 'cause we're cool) includes a sandy beach, rocky tide pools, and stands of sycamore and oak trees along El Capitán Creek. It's a perfect setting for swimming, fishing, surfing, picnicking, and camping. A stairway provides access from the low bluffs to the beach area. Amenities include RV hookups, pay showers, clean restrooms, hiking and bike trails, a seasonal general store with bait and tackle, a half-mile nature trail (with an elevation gain of a whopping eighteen feet!), and several grassy areas with picnic tables and fire pits. There is beach access, but camping isn't allowed on the actual beach. It's very woodsy here, with lots of low brush and mature trees. There is also poison oak, so watch out. There are four twenty-minute parking spaces to the right directly after the guard entrance. If no one is manning the booth, it's a paid honor system. If someone is there, it's a $10 day-use fee even for the free twenty-minute parking. That stinks. Take Highway 101 until you reach the El Capitán signs. Exit and head toward the ocean. The road will take you right into the park.

### Surfing

Surfers are a protective lot; they don't want you horning in on their special breaks. Nonetheless, Santa Barbara has many prime surf spots. The best time to surf is winter, followed by fall. The primary swells are from storms in the North Pacific, which generate waves as they approach the West Coast. Spring swells tend to be wind generated and less powerful.

**The Rincon** is the undisputed king of the surf spots, with a large point break. Rincon straddles Ventura and Santa Barbara counties and gets insanely crowded. A long right point break with several distinct lineups means that if you can connect the entire point, it's a ride over a mile long. Exit Highway 101 at Bates Road (going north or south) and park in either the county or state lot.

By contrast, **Leadbetter Point** near City College has small, fun, easy waves that are good for beginners. There are a lot of peaks along this small right point break. Take Cabrillo Boulevard past Stearns Wharf and turn left into the pay parking lot.

**Campus Point**, Isla Vista Cliffs, is located at UCSB on the eastern edge of campus. There's a small right point break with a small beach break, and the cliffs lead west to Devereux Point, another right with many peaks. It gets crowded sometimes because students simply cross the street from their dorms and hit the waves. There are also lots of longboarders, and there's a lot of tar from natural oil upwellings near the aptly named Coal Oil Point.

If surfing is new to you and you want to brush up on your skills, or if you want to learn while you're in town, **Surf Happens Surf School** (surfhappens.com, 805/966-3613) will teach you the basics individually, as a couple, or even as a team-building exercise.

## Whale Watching and Sunset Cruises

There's nothing like the awesomeness of seeing a whale or a pod of dolphins, or the tranquil simplicity of a sunset, from the deck of a boat. I strongly suggest a sunset cruise when you visit, regardless of whom you book with. The views back to the city are amazing, and it"s always time for a cool change (thanks, Little River Band!).

**Sunset Kidd Sailing** (sunsetkidd.com, 805/962-8222) offers private charters and morning, afternoon, and evening cruises on its forty-one-foot sailing yacht. It's a great ship, holding only fifteen people. Typically, the Sunset Kidd will motor out to wherever, and then it generally cuts the motor and rigs the sails for a quiet return to the harbor. But remember, this is a sailboat, therefore there's a lot of up and down movement.

**Condor Express** (condorexpress.com, 805/882-0088) has a high-speed catamaran, which means you're tooling on the water quickly, not sailing. This is a more stable ride for those prone to motion sickness. It offers a full roster of cruises and excursions.

## Kayaking and Stand-Up Paddle Boarding

If you launch from the harbor and pass the breakwater, a half mile straight out is a green buoy that is usually packed with seals basking in the sun. Making a slow approach, you can easily get within five feet. Otherwise, enjoy the coast, but remember it's easy to paddle out and always longer to come back. Winds, currents, and just being tired mean you could end up with a longer day than you had planned. Keep hydrated and use sun protection.

**The Paddle Sports Center** (www.paddlesportsca.com, 117 Harbor Way, 805/617-3425) has been around for twenty years and has a great staff. You can rent gear and get trained in both kayaking and paddle surfing.

## Scuba

The Channel Islands are some of the best dive spots on the Western Seaboard. I have dove (dived? diven?) at Anacapa and Santa Cruz and know firsthand that the confluence of warm tropical water and cooler waters allows for a large variety of fish and plant life. We have some very cool kelp beds, which are way awesome to dive in. The islands are a great day trip, usually allowing for three to four tank dives. Other divers prefer an ocean entrance, and you'll often see divers enter the surf breaks right off shore. The visibility can be pretty limited as there is a long shelf, but on clear days without much surge you can still find a lot of sea life just twenty yards off shore.

**Peace Boat** (peaceboat.com, 1691 Spinnaker Dr., G Dock, Ventura, 805/650-3483) is the company I prefer to scuba with, even though it launches out of Ventura, thirty minutes south of Santa Barbara. The Peace is a sixty-five-foot dive boat whose staff members are certified, and the boat is equipped for Nitrox. The Peace Boat has a very conscientious staff who know the waters and emergency procedures. Plus, on the way back from a four-tank dive, you can soak in the hot tub while having ice cream—it's the perfect ending to a long day of diving.

## Sites: Historic

**Andree Clark Bird Refuge** (1400 E. Cabrillo Blvd., 805/564-5418) This is a forty-two-acre salt marsh with a few wooden benches around the perimeter, hidden by tall reeds. For birders, this is an excellent spot to see white pelicans, black-crowned night herons, egrets and bushtits, grebes and mallards. Once considered a viable location to put the harbor, the naturally protected cove was quickly overlooked because early yachts wouldn't have fit inside. It sounds like a respite, what with the word "refuge" in the title; the birds love the open water and reeds, and so will you. But it's sandwiched between busy Cabrillo Boulevard, the 101 freeway, and the train tracks. Regardless, in the early mornings, as the mist rises from the lake, it's rather tranquil.

**Moreton Bay Fig Tree** (Montecito and Chapala Streets) With roots that are six feet tall above ground, this stunning tree planted in 1877—and nearly lost forever when they decided to chop it down—is one of the largest trees of its kind in California. Transplanted from its original site on State Street by a young girl named Adeline Crabb (crabb tree?), the cutting came from Australia. The tree was designated a California Historical Landmark in 1970 and is on the register of Big Trees. This baby is 80 feet high and spreads 198 feet across. The trunk diameter is more than twelve feet. You can't climb on it, but the short amount of time needed to see it will be well worth it. This stunning tree is located behind the train station off Montecito Street.

**Casa de la Guerra** (sbthp.org, 15 E. De La Guerra St., 805/965-0093, $5, includes admission to the Presidio) The Casa (house) has been at the heart of Santa Barbara's history since its construction between 1819 and 1827 by the fifth Presidio commander, Jose de la Guerra. Among Santa Barbara's wealthiest and most influential citizens, De La Guerra was the town's father figure of sorts, meaning that Casa de la Guerra became the social, political, and cultural center of the small pueblo of Santa Barbara. Sadly, I was never invited to any of the festivities. The De La Guerra legacy continued with the political activity of De La Guerra's son, Pablo, during the early years of California's statehood. Pablo served as a state senator and as lieutenant governor of the state. In 1874, the first City Hall was constructed opposite the Casa in Plaza de la Guerra. In 1922, El Paseo, a meandering shopping street, was designed and built around the Casa. When the first Old Spanish Days Fiesta was held in 1924, parties and dances were held at

Casa de la Guerra in the large courtyard; you can stand there now, but without the party. Multiple rooms in the house show how the "wealthy" of the time lived—you know, hardwood floors and all.

**Doremus Stone Pine Trees** (300-800 blocks of Anacapa Street) So named for Augustus Doremus, the city's first parks superintendent, these magnificent trees were planted between 1908 and 1929 and form an incredible canopy shielding us from the sun and sky. Vast in their reach and sublime in their simplicity, the sixty-foot trees are worthy of a visit, even just a drive down Anacapa. Look up, but keep your eyes on the road.

**El Presidio de Santa Barbara State Historic Park** (sbthp. org, 123 E. Canon Perdido St., 805/965-0093, $5, includes admission to Casa de la Guerra) This is the birthplace of Santa Barbara. The Presidio, a military fort, was founded April 21, 1782, under the rule of King Carlos III of Spain; there's a statue of him in the interior courtyard, a gift from Spain to Santa Barbara—he looks like George Washington to me. This presidio was the last in a chain of four military fortresses built by the Spanish along the coast of California. The whitewashed buildings were constructed of sun-dried adobe bricks laid on foundations of sandstone boulders. Timbers from the Los Padres mountains supported roofs of red tile. In the old days, the red tiles of the roofs here were made by plastering the top of a woman's leg; you'll notice that the old tiles are narrow at one end and broaden at the other, the dimensions from a woman's knee up to her hip. The

*Making modern-day adobe at the Presidio*

buildings of the Presidio formed a quadrangle enclosing a central parade ground, the whole thing surrounded by an outer defense wall with two cannon bastions. The most prominent structure was, and still is, the chapel, Santa Barbara's very first church for its townspeople. The Christianized Chumash population worshipped at the mission up the road.

Today, only two sections of the original Presidio quadrangle remain. The first is the Visitors Center portion, and the second is El Cuartel, the family residence of the soldier assigned to guard the western gate. Though many of the Presidio buildings have been reconstructed, El Cuartel (built in 1782, and thus the second-oldest building in all of California), right across the street from the chapel, is a great example of living architecture. The massive walls still stand as they have for more than 230 years, and it's just so cool to experience this—to walk into the home and understand the powerful nature of simple buildings to communicate about the past. El Cuartel is small, with tiny doors and windows, but it's awesome to stand in the exact spot where history happened and feel the connection. El Cuartel was used as a private residence up to the 1940s. A visit to the Presidio includes several rooms featuring adobe, pottery, sculpture, and cannons. With the Presidio the way it is now, people don't realize how large the original fort was. Kitty corner is Panino—good sandwiches, to be sure, but in the back parking lot are striped lines showing where the presidio walls extended to. It's here that you get an idea of how large the building was; for reasons unknown, no one tells you about this.

**Faith Mission Building** (409 State St.) This is currently known as the Blind Tiger. But this building, one of the oldest on State Street, opened its doors in 1889 to convert men "from their erring ways." The good intentions, however, didn't allow the church to stay open for long, and the building became a hotel in 1931. It's been a sushi joint with pool tables and stiff drinks, it's seen burlesque shows, and there is an adult bookstore two doors away. No doubt the former parishioners are rolling in their graves, as there's probably a lot of "erring" going on these days. Even if you don't go inside, at least appreciate the exterior.

**Fithian Building** (629 State St.) Walk by this building and you may not think much of it. Pedestrian stores front the street, and aside from a small historic plaque it's barely worth noticing, right? Do yourself a favor and enter the double doors and go to the top of the stairs. You'll be treated to a beautifully restored turn-of-the-century interior, complete with original hardwood floors, narrow offices, and doorways with transoms. Built in 1895, the exterior doesn't do justice to the interior. Now a collection of architects' and designers' offices, it's a blast from the past and worth a few minutes to see how much has changed.

**Old Mission Santa Barbara** (santabarbaramission.org, 2201 Laguna St., 805/682-4713, $5) The mission is more closely associated with Santa Barbara than any other landmark. Known as the Queen of the Missions (OK, who came up

*Old Mission Santa Barbara, 1905*

*Old Mission Santa Barbara today*

with that one?), it was founded on December 4, 1786, the feast day of Saint Barbara. Originally there were no plans to place the mission on this spot, but after considering the proximity to a fresh water source, namely Mission Creek, and the defensible position of being able to view the ocean in time to see unfriendly ships approaching, it was decided the area was ideal. You know what they say: location, location, location. Though visually striking, it's one of the least authentic-looking of the missions. The original adobe church was a simple structure, enlarged two times to accommodate growth. The fourth church iteration, which is the current one, was built in 1820. The 1925 earthquake inflicted major damage on the mission, and the east bell tower was almost completely destroyed; its twin tower (that's not a Tolkien reference) sustained serious injury, and restoration efforts began in May 1926. Within ten years, signs of further problems began to appear. Cracks emerged in the mission towers and facade, and the conditions continued to worsen, so that by 1949 it was apparent that something desperately needed to be done. Studies revealed that chemical reactions inside the concrete were fatally weakening the material, rendering the building unsafe. Drastic action was called for—a total reconstruction of both the towers and the facade. Work began in 1950 and continued until the summer of 1953. What you see today is the culmination of decades of restoration efforts.

In addition to exploring the interior church, you can view the padre's quarters and the kitchen. The cemetery is behind the mission and concludes the self-guided tour. While there, walk across the lawn to the rose garden, where more than a thousand different varieties are growing. As you walk across the street, remind yourself that this was where some of the grapevines were planted. Still an active church, this has been a gathering spot for more than 230 years. Also across the street, where most visitors don't go, are more remnants from the early mission days. Eight partial structures still stand, including a low stone wall, which was the original aqueduct, as well as the tannery vat and stone-walled prison. Farther up the street are the upper and lower reservoirs, the water filter house (which used a sophisticated system of filtering water through rocks and sand to purify it), and a pottery shed from 1808 where women made the red tiles for the roofs. Lastly, make sure you stand on the mission steps looking out to the ocean. From this spot you get a clearer idea of the vantage point the mission had to see incoming ships and why the mission was built here.

**Painted Cave** (Painted Cave Rd., off Highway 154) This is literally the smallest state park you'll ever visit. Parking stinks, as you're on a windy road, so be careful. A short flight of stairs takes you to a cave, and inside are actual paintings by local Chumash Indians from the 1600s, maybe earlier. Okay, maybe "paintings" conjures up images of Monet. These are cave drawings, symbols, and petroglyphs, not nuanced postmodern still lifes. Take a flashlight with you so you can really see the bold colors and cool images drawn onto the sandstone cave walls. A fence separates you from the paintings since damage has been done to them over the years, but it's only 15 feet that separates you from history. Check it out. It won't take long, but it's pretty impressive. From Highway 154, take Painted Cave Road up two miles; the cave is on your left.

**Santa Barbara Cemetery** (901 Channel Dr., 805/969-3231) The final resting place of the dead isn't your usual stop when you visit a new place (though admittedly I routinely visit cemeteries all over the world). The cemetery is certainly quiet and sits on the best piece of land, high on a bluff overlooking the Pacific Ocean, with pristine views to the mountains and Channel Islands (not together—you have to look both ways). As cemeteries go, this is flat-out beautiful. Many notables from Santa Barbara history are buried here, as are actors Ronald Colman and Fess Parker and a few tragic souls from the legendary Jonestown massacre in Guyana in 1978; otherwise, you've probably never heard of these folks. The land goes back to 1867 as a burial place. There's even a two-hundred-page book on the complete history of the cemetery, *The Best Last Place*. Such is the dedication of Santa Barbara natives and their love of local history . . . and burials, I guess. A short walk across the thin grass amid palm trees and headstones will give you a new perspective on life—if not, go wine tasting.

**Santa Barbara County Courthouse** (sbcourts.org, 1100 Anacapa St., 805/882-4520) This building has been called the most beautiful public building in America, and it is, period. Covering an entire block, the courthouse is a stunning example of Spanish and Moorish designs, not Mexican as is often believed. William Mooser designed this courthouse to replace the earlier 1872 version, a Colonial-looking thing with a massive domed cupola. When the courthouse was completed in 1929, it was unlike anything in the city, or any city. Lush grounds, including the copious lawn and Sunken Gardens, set the stage for this sandstone building. Everywhere you look there are arabesque windows, archways, hand-painted wood ceilings and walls

*The county courthouse coaxes callers continuously.*

with intricate designs, hand-painted tile inlays flashing brilliant colors, and native designs. Of particular note is the mural room, once used for the county board of supervisors. The huge room is covered in a mural depicting the early Chumash people and following the history of the area toward California statehood.

The clocktower, known as El Mirador, is one of the tallest structures in the city, a mere eighty-five feet, but it is here where you will get the best views of downtown's ubiquitous red-tiled roofs, as well as the mountains and ocean from a downtown perspective. Take the elevator to the fourth floor. There, a dozen steps lead up and out to the platform. You'll be thrilled at the views splayed out in front of you. Placards describe points of interest in each direction so you can easily get your bearings. This is a must photo op. This is also still a functioning courthouse. I know this all too well, as I served on jury duty here (please don't ask; it was a crappy experience). You don't need the formal tour to appreciate the sheer beauty and craftsmanship of the building, but it will give you more specific information. Ironically, by the county's current building codes and standards, the courthouse could never be approved and built today. This is the single best example of Santa Barbara, more so than the mission and the wharf. If you have limited time, come here.

**Santa Barbara Zoological Gardens** (santabarbarazoo.org, 500 Ninos Dr., 805/962-5339, $17) In the early 1960s, a group of locals decided the city needed a zoo. With little more than time in one hand and a hammer in the other, they constructed the Santa Barbara Zoo on a prime plot of thirty acres overlooking the ocean. Today the zoo, small and intimate and in some ways old-fashioned looking, is a testament to citizens banding together. The zoological garden sits on the former estate of Lillian Child, a wealthy woman who built lush gardens, and many of the trees date back to the 1920s. Child routinely allowed hobos (now we call them homeless) to camp on her property, and they built a small, ramshackle village on what is now the parking lot. Part of the beauty of the zoo is that it's small enough to see the animals up close. It has been called the "Audrey Hepburn of zoos": small but sophisticated. The zoo brags that it is the only one where lions have views of beach volleyball. True enough, but so do the giraffes. The zoo features beautifully landscaped gardens and views to the ocean, the Andree Clark Bird Refuge, and the mountains. You can see condors, bald eagles, and the adorable Channel Islands fox, along with other

*The Channel Islands fox, photographed on Santa Cruz Island*

native animals and plants from the Channel Islands and surrounding mountains.

## Sites: Not Exactly Historic

**Frog Wall** (1600 block of Paterna Rd.) Also known as the Frog Shrine, this is one of those weird, cool, and highly unknown things that is totally unique to Santa Barbara. In 1986 a woman saw a plastic frog placed along an old sandstone wall in her neigh-borhood on what's called the Riviera. She's not sure why she did what she did, but she found a plastic frog and placed it next to the first one. A few days later, a third frog appeared. Then more frog paraphernalia appeared: PEZ dispenser frogs, soap-on-a-rope frogs, stuffed frogs, metallic frogs, clock frogs, garden orna-ment frogs, stickers, photos,

*The Frog Wall*

anything and everything to do with frogs. Now the frog wall is a local landmark, so under the radar that most people who live in Santa Barbara have never been here or even heard of it. Bring a frog and take nothing away, as I have done. Hop to it.

**Goleta Butterfly Grove** (goletabutterflygrove.com, 7559 Palos Verdes Dr., Goleta, 805/961-7571) Monarchs (the butterflies, not royalty) are usually found in Goleta from mid-November through mid-February, and docents are available on weekends from 11 a.m. to 2 p.m. during these months. This is the smallest of the three groves along the Central Coast (Pacific Grove in Monterey and Pismo Beach in San Luis Obispo are the other two). It is open every day during daylight hours, and it's free. The short lifespan of these silent, beautiful creatures is remarkable. Goleta Butterfly Grove is in the Sperling Preserve on the Ellwood Mesa in Goleta, just north of downtown Santa Barbara. Free parking is available.

**Knapp's Castle** (Note: This is not a typical tourist site; it's actually private property with no address or phone, though accessible to the public) In 1916, George Owen Knapp, founder of Union Carbide, which has become a behemoth chemical monopoly, purchased a 160-acre parcel, including a ridgeline, in the mountains overlooking the Valley. He built a seven-building complex he called the Lodge at San Marcos, not really a castle at all. Knapp already owned the seventy-acre Arcady estate in Montecito but wanted a more rustic country home, in contrast to his immaculate estate—must be nice. The laborious efforts to build the lodge took years, given the relative isolation of the property and the difficulty of hauling materials into the mountains. In 1940, Frances Holden bought the property from Knapp,

*Knapp's Castle, and one of my wedding photos. Photo by Kevin Rolly*

59

no doubt looking forward to many long years of peace and quiet in the remote home. But fate had other plans, and just five weeks later the entire property was destroyed by a forest fire. Now only some of the massive sandstone foundations, fireplace pillars, arches, and walls remain intact. It is hauntingly beautiful and rugged, and often only the whisper of the wind through the trees can be heard. The parcel is still privately owned but open to the public. To access it, turn onto East Camino Cielo at the top of the San Marcos Pass and drive exactly three miles. On your left will be a rusted gate. From there it's approximately a ten-minute walk to the property. As you slowly descend off the road you'll begin to see the tops of the fireplaces, like sentinels standing guard in the distance. Knapp's Castle is a popular place for photo shoots (my wife and I shot wedding photos here) and picnics and has amazing views. It's actually impossible to get a bad photo here, and that's good news for any shutterbug.

## Eat AND Drink

### Bars

Every city needs its watering holes. Plenty of bars clog a two-block section of State Street, and more hug the side streets. But this is nothing unusual. Of the first fifty business licenses issued by the newly established city of Santa Barbara in 1850, thirty-two were for saloons, and we haven't stopped drinking since. Known as the **State Street Crawl**, the 400 to 600 blocks of State Street are where the majority of bars are located. Frequented mainly by college students, this area has become a hot spot on weekends for cheap drinks and short skirts. All bars close at 2 a.m., and this is often when trouble occurs, especially on weekends. Fights are common because far too many intoxicated people converge at the same time. Many bars in Santa Barbara

60

are nothing special, just the tedious scent of stale beer and chlorine mops. Therefore, check out these spots.

**Joe's Café** (joescafesb.com, 536 State St., 805/966-4638) Joe's arguably serves some of the stiffest drinks in town, which is why it is so popular. It's primarily a restaurant with okay food, but the bar action is constant. There's an old-school feel to the place, harkening back to its 1920 origins, making it one of the oldest restaurants and bars in town. It gets packed here on weekends. For a completely irrelevant distinction, it is one of the only places to have a hanging neon sign out front.

**James Joyce** (sbjamesjoyce.com, 513 State St., 805/962-2688) The writer James Joyce never visited Santa Barbara, but the bar named after him offers free darts and free peanuts, and the Guinness comes quickly from the tap. There is a great beer and whiskey selection, as well. The walls are lined with photos of, we assume, Irishmen, and the tin ceiling and rugged feel of the place, not to mention the nice fireplace, mean there's usually an older crowd here. A small dance floor in the back doesn't get much use, but the wood bar is a classic drinking spot.

**Uptown Lounge** (sbuptownlounge.com, 3126 State St., 805/845-8800) This is that neighborhood bar that's respectable—not too divey or too stuffy. Located away from downtown, it offers plenty of food, such as dogs, wings, salads, and pizza. Forget the wines and beers and go for the stiff stuff, while playing pool.

## Coffee and Other Stimulants

**Santa Barbara Roasting Company** (sbcoffee.com, 321 Motor Way, 805/962-5213) Roasting its own style of beans with names like Santa Barbara Blend and State Street Blend, all in a really cool exposed-brick space, RoCo (as we call it) has free wireless Internet, and it sells a few baked goods (not really worth it). Most people come here for a casual meeting, a good cup of joe at a good price, and the heady aroma of roasting coffee beans in the next room. The staff has long been slow and often un-helpful, but once you get your coffee you're within walking distance of the beach.

**Vices and Spices** (vicesandspices.net, 3558 State St., 805/687-7196) This small neighborhood spot has been quietly brewing teas and making coffee for forty-two years under the same ownership. It doesn't draw the pretentious crowd with its fancy caramel/soy/mocha/frothy/goat-milk concoctions. Nay, nay. This is an under-the-radar, quiet environment for people who are serious about their tea and coffee. It sells fifty different bulk teas (also available by the cup), bulk spices like juniper berries and fenugreek (seriously?), and lots of coffee. This is where I buy my French roast.

## Restaurants and Food

You may have heard the claim that Santa Barbara has more restaurants per capita than any other city its size in the US (a rumor probably started by a restaurant owner). Who cares whether it's true? What you want is the best a city can offer, *not* the touristy, benign, overpriced food you'll find everywhere—and, yes, we have our share of that. From taco stands to five-star restaurants, we've got it. Please avoid coupons from free magazines; those spots are average at best. Weirdly, the waterfront is a collection of average restaurants with great views, so don't be sucked in by the allure of seeing the beach while you eat. Visit the places outlined here.

### American-ish

**Angel Oak** $$$$, L-D (angeloaksb.com, 8301 Hollister Ave., Goleta, 877/968-0100) The signature restaurant at the

Bacara Resort isn't as exclusive as it sounds. After many iterations and names, this place has hit its stride. Hip and cool lights hang from the bar like little orbs of moonlight. It's dark and moody at night, less so during the day when your views are the entire Pacific Ocean. If nothing else, get the lobster bisque with saffron rouille, so rich and potent you can smell it before it arrives. Poured tableside, it is tremendous. Also, the filet—staggeringly tender, beautifully and, yes, lovingly cooked. Though I'm not a fan of asparagus, the pan-seared jumbo asparagus with Meyer lemon beurre blanc is pretty impressive.

**Cold Spring Tavern** $$, B-L-D (coldspringtavern.com, 5995 Stagecoach Rd., 805/967-0066) This former stagecoach stop, built in 1886, is rustic and used to be secluded. There's a restaurant on site and live music on the weekends, as well as bikers, townies, and everyone in between. A stream runs by the place, which is situated in a narrow canyon, and it can be cold even during the summer. There is often dancing both inside and outside the bar. The on-site restaurant, in a separate building, is the place to find tri-tip sandwiches during the summer, grilled outdoors over an open flame. But the tavern is best known for wild game, including rabbit, venison, and boar, and very good chili. A visit here is as much about the food as it is about just being in the charming space. There's an old jail on site, as well, a one-room wood building that used to hold unruly customers. If you don't pay your bill, you might end up there (hint: it's pretty easy to escape).

**Farmer Boy** $, B-L-D (farmerboy.com, 3427 State St., 805/845-6749) This is one of the oldest restaurants in town (it opened in 1958), and new owners took over a few years back and recreated the classic diner. It's best known for its cinnamon rolls, which are about the size of a farmer's boy—they are enough for two people, and ya gotta get one. The menu jokes, "Add paramedics w/ defibrillator,

$2,300." Also great are the chicken-fried biscuit sliders, a terrific soup pozole verde, and Cobb salad. Stop in and get the real feel for a '50s diner. Yes, breakfast is served all day.

**Finch & Fork** $$$, B-L-D (finchandforkrestaurant.com, 31 W. Carrillo Blvd., 805/879-9100) Most hotel restaurants are forgettable, but this birdie sings. Chef James Siao creates seasonal menus reflective of the diversity of Santa Barbara and uses just six ingredients per dish to maximize flavor. There are multiple wood-toned dining areas with both booths and tables. It's open without being noisy—large yet intimate. The fried-chicken sliders with cilantro slaw and smoked honey mustard are wonderfully light, moist, and crisp. The roasted cauliflower skillet is a mix of tender cauliflower, broccoli, and roasted capers. Recommended are the chili-caramel pork ribs and the best carrot cake I've ever had (and I don't like carrot cake). There's a terrific cocktail program, too.

**John Dunn Gourmet Dining Room** $$, L-D (Santa Barbara City College, 805/965-0581 x 2773) This is unique. Imagine a restaurant where you must have reservations, the menu is limited, parking is a pain, and your wait staff and cooks are all kids. Well, not exactly. The Culinary Arts program at Santa Barbara City College offers lunches and four-course dinners (dinners come with wine pairings), all designed, cooked, and served by those in the program, who even come up with the menu. The food is quite good, and this is so under the radar that most locals don't even know about it. The menus change weekly, so help someone get an easy "A."

**Seven Bar & Kitchen** $, D-Sunday brunch (sevensb.com, 224 Helena Ave., 805/845-0377) Seven has long been considered an ideal number, but restaurants in Santa Barbara are anything but assured success, regardless of numerology. So when Seven opened in the Funk Zone, it focused on its food, not gimmicks; fortunately for this town, we have one more cool, hip eatery. A central bar flanks two separate dining areas that have exposed brick walls; rotating local art hugs the walls. There's a small outdoor patio for more seclusion and better weather. Seven makes terrific cocktails, many using local ingredients. Food-wise, you've gotta go with the chicken and waffles—small chunks of battered, fried chicken infused with maple and then covered with a full-sized waffle. Also good are the pulled-pork sliders (pork, cabbage, and a cilantro slaw) and sandwiches named for, what else, the seven deadly sins. Lord have mercy!

**Wildwood Kitchen** $$, L-D (wildwoodkitchensb.com, 410 E. Haley St., 805/845-3995) Smoked meats are what it's all about at Wildwood. Pulled pork is the signature sandwich, topped with pickles and coleslaw on a grilled bun. Yes, it's as good as it sounds. Wildwood makes everything from scratch, including its BBQ sauces—jalapeño, coffee, mustard, and beer. The cornbread is also a must, so moist and tender you'll think you're in Iowa. There's also the you-gotta-try-it-once Frito pie, brisket, and lots of other meats. There's a back patio, and inside it's rustic and tame.

### Burgers and Sandwiches

**Metropulos** $, L (metrofinefoods.com, 216 E. Yanonali St., 805/899-2300) Just one block from the beach, this is the best place to gather picnic supplies. Get a sandwich or salad to go, or some of the many olives from Africa, Spain, and Italy. The sandwiches are wonderful—for example, the apple-ham-brie panini on multigrain sourdough. Or, try one of my favorite combinations, a cranberry goat-cheese salad with spinach and organic mixed greens. It also has a small wine shop, colorful and creative pastas to take home and cook (as I have done), and a really moist chocolate biscotti. The handful of outdoor seats are prime real estate.

**The Shop Café** $, B-L (730 N. Milpas, 805/845-1696) This neighborhood café started when the owners, who live close by, wanted someplace to get coffee and good food; the Milpas corridor is mainly Mexican food joints. Thus, this former taqueria turned hot-dog stand has been repurposed into a delightful urban coffee shop. Look for the General Sanders—buttermilk fried chicken with tarragon mayonnaise and a slaw of cabbage, apple slices, and pickled onions, all piled onto a bun. Or try the McQueen, a quiche made with scallions, black beans, corn, tomato sauce, and cheddar cheese, and then topped with sliced fresh tomatoes. The café bakes its own pastries and cookies, and the brown-butter cookie wins.

**State & Fig** $$, B-L (stateandfig.com, 1114 State St., 805/965-1730) Tucked into La Arcada Court but worth seeking out, State & Fig serves breakfasts that include the Figg'in Toast—fig cream cheese layered between French toast, served with house-made sausage and topped with vanilla maple syrup. Enough said. The Fig Burger is another dish using the signature fig, in this case as a fig jam, with bacon, arugula, bleu cheese, and caramelized onions on a toasted bun. Not everything has fig, mind you, so don't be alarmed. The food is terrific, but the service is a little off. Fig'ures.

**South Coast Deli** $, B-L (southcoastdeli.com, 1436 Chapala St., 805/560-9800) This deli has several locations around town and is an excellent choice for breakfast sandwiches, salads, and lunches. I love the Phatty, your basic chicken salad with bacon, avocado, and basil mayo, though I hate the name. Or, wake up to Max's breakfast sammie, which consists of scrambled eggs, bacon, tomato, pepper-jack cheese, and a garlic-Tabasco mayonnaise on grilled sourdough bread—a little heat to start your day. The terrific food here is well priced, amazingly consistent, and packed with flavors, and the staff are properly trained—exactly what you want in a deli.

**The Habit Burger Grill** $, L-D (habitburger.com, 5735 Hollister Ave., Goleta, 805/964-0366) Assuming you've read this book carefully, you might see this and say, "Hey, I thought you said no chain restaurants." And yes, technically you'd be correct, Mr. Smarty. But this spot is where the Habit started in 1969. So, yeah, it's a chain, but this is the original. You'll find great burgers and a grilled chicken Caesar salad, and this is the only place to offer a chili cheeseburger (not on the menu). The food is inexpensive and darn tasty. There are now more than 150 locations in California alone (not to mention Arizona, Utah, Florida, New Jersey, and Dubai!). It's a limited menu, and at lunch and dinner all the locations are always crowded . . . but there are reasons for this!

**The Lark** $$, L-D (thelarksb.com, 131 Anacapa St., 805/284-0370) The Lark, named for an overnight Pullman train that serviced Santa Barbara for sixty years, is not a lark. It's become one of the town's hottest spots, but it also lives up to the hype. A strong cocktail and wine program leads to some killer dishes, such as crispy fried brussels sprouts (go ahead, make the face, it's OK) mixed with Medjool dates, sesame, lime, and garum for a savory element. I love the absurdly wonderful caramelized cauliflower gratin baked with Gruyere cheese, preserved lemon, chili flakes, and bacon breadcrumbs. The rosemary chicken and kale salad (yes, kale is sooo trendy right now) are winners. Reservations are a must for both indoor and outdoor seating. The Lark has quickly become an institution.

### Bakeries

Julia Child (who lived in Santa Barbara during her last years) once said, "How can a nation be great if its bread tastes like Kleenex?"

Um . . . I don't know, Julia. But her comment is nothing to sneeze at.

**Helena Avenue Bakery** $$, B-L (helenaavenuebakery.com, 131 Anacapa St., Suite C, 805/880-3383) This bakery has a two-pronged approach: bakery treats and picnic lunches. The bakery offers various quiche selections with a deftly crispy crust, baguettes, walnut batards, and ciabatta bread, not to mention egg croissants with arugula pesto and pro- sciutto, apricot-thyme croissants, and cookies made with the bakery's rich peanut butter. But there is also the Picnic Counter, offering prepared foods for take-away, such as house-pickled veggies; couscous salad with cherry toma- toes, cucumber, and feta cheese; brussels sprouts Caesar salad; focaccia with roasted corn, pasilla peppers, queso fresco, and cilantro; and a fried-chicken sandwich on ciabatta.

**Renaud's** $, L-D (renaudsbakery.com, 1324 State St., 805/892-2800; 3315 State St., 805/569-2400) I've always been a fan of Renaud's. After all, it's a French guy making French pastries. Ooh-la-la. Prior to his opening in 2008, Santa Barbara really didn't have anything much resembling authentic French pastries. His croissant is, as you should rightfully assume, near perfection. Light, crisp, and loaded with butter, it's messy but spot on. The chocolate croissant isn't quite as light and flaky as its counterpart but is still butter-rich, with chunks of chocolate layered into it. The apricot tart, like many of his fruit tarts, has a light, flaky, and crispy crust. The bakery does breakfasts and lunches, as well, so if you're feeling Parisian, this is a great stop. Two locations, one on mid-State and one on Upper State Street, make it easier.

### Chinese

**China Pavilion** $$, L-D (china-pavilion.com, 1202 Chapala St., 805/560-6028) These folks offer a comprehensive lunch and dinner menu, dim sum, and Chinese New Year specialties, and the food is quite good. I love the Ants on the Tree—sautéed pork atop crunchy bean thread noodles—and the spicy basil eggplant. There are plenty of vegetarian options, as well, and the décor is elegant without being cheesy or stuffy.

**Shang Hai** $, L-D (shanghaisbca.net, 830 N. Milpas St., 805/962-7833) Tucked into a forgettable corner strip mall, this Chinese restaurant has been around for more than thirty years. One of the reasons Shang Hai is popular, apart from the very good food, is that there is a huge variety of vegetarian choices, and the restaurant doesn't use any MSG in its dishes. The corn egg-drop soup, garlic lamb, and tofu and vegetables with curry sauce are just a few of the massive number of choices. The service is focused and rapid, and the food is flavorful, fresh, and creative.

### Chocolates and Sweets

Chocolate was a staple during the Mission period, and mission documents from 1779 through 1810 record the importance of chocolate. The padres routinely drank hot chocolate first thing in the morning before breakfast. Even Father Junipero Serra, who founded Old Mission Santa Barbara, wrote about chocolate in the early 1770s. But chocolate was constantly ordered in large quantities and was requested specifically from Caracas and Tabasco, Mexico, confirming the concept that every place produces a product specific to its inherent ecology. Specific pots were associated with chocolate, many with locking lids because of the value of the cocoa they contained. The *jerro chocolatero* pots were made from copper and used to heat and then whip the chocolate into a drink. These days it's way easier to be a chocoholic by simply visiting these guys.

**Chocolate Maya** (chocolatemaya.com, 15 W. Gutierrez St., 805/965-5956) Here you'll find an assortment of chocolates from across the globe, including some made on site. It's all things chocolate, and the staff will put together a special chocolate tasting if you contact them in advance. These are great gift items in that there are playful molded chocolates of great quality, standard bars, and all sorts of cool shapes. You'll find all types of cocoa (except Coco Chanel).

**Jessica Foster Confections** (jessicafosterconfections.com, 805/637-6985) Say chocolate in Santa Barbara and most people think Jessica Foster. Foster started her company after working as a pastry chef at a local restaurant. She had no formal training but has created a very successful business. She hand rolls and hand dips thirty different flavors. You can find her truffles at Lazy Acres, Whole Foods, and Pierre Lafond in Montecito. But what exactly is a truffle? "It's really a ganache-filled bonbon," Foster says; they have nothing to do with the truffles dug up from the ground. She ships throughout the US but also takes appointments in her small kitchen. If you're so inclined, she offers a quarterly chocolate club (uh, yes). Milk chocolate with sea salt and pepper, as well as white chocolate Meyer lemon, are her top-selling truffles. During Halloween she makes these really cool chocolate skulls.

**Twenty-Four Blackbirds** (twentyfourblackbirds.com, 615 De La Vina St., 831/566-2643) The only bean-to-bar guy in town, Mike Orlando buys, roasts, and makes chocolate bars directly from the cocoa bean. Now, I should tell you, this is for you hardcore chocolate lovers for whom bitter is best. You can find his bars all over town. They ain't cheap, but they are clean, pure expressions of chocolate. Orlando buys raw beans from places like Peru, Madagascar, and the Dominican Republic, roasts them, crushes them, refines them, and molds them into bars. It's a time-consuming process, and he is one of the few people in the US to make chocolate by hand. A former analytical chemist at UCSB, he's well adapted to the specificity of the tedious process. What you get is cocoa and sugar—that's it. The chocolate bars are hand signed by lot number and expiration date. His chocolate is probably the purest expression of original cocoa—deep and bittersweet.

*Mike Orlando and his bean-to-bar chocolate bars*

## Farmers Markets

Farmers markets are a dime a dozen, and you can find them in any city. Therefore, they need to have an intrinsic value. Santa Barbara has six of them, and they are just as much about being social as getting lemon basil or torpedo onions. You're likely to see local chefs scouring the stalls for what they want to put on your plate that evening. Check out sbfarmersmarket.org for a complete schedule. These two are the best.

**The Saturday Farmers Market** (Santa Barbara and Cota Streets, 8:30 a.m. to 12:30 p.m.) is the granddaddy. Held in a parking lot, it offers local produce and products such as honey, fruits and veggies, and nuts. If Saturday is the social gathering, then the **Tuesday afternoon State Street market** (500-600 blocks of State Street) is the place to be seen—a hip organic stroll in town right on the main drag, with a Hollywood vibe. This iteration covers several blocks and is conveniently located near multiple bars in case you need some social lubricant after consuming one too many organic sunflower seeds.

## Greek

**Yanni's Greek & American Deli** $, L (3102 State St., 805/682-2051) This place looks uninviting from the outside, and you're not sure just what's going on in there. Be calm: it's Greek food, made by Greek people. The real Greek salad is so loaded with stuff it will make your head spin just like Greece's debt crisis. Everything in this salad is large, crunchy, and cut and prepared when you order it. The Greek gyro of lamb and beef with diced tomatoes, fresh dill, red onion, and house-made tzatziki sauce, wrapped in pita bread, is immensely flavorful and true to the Greek tradition. The house-made baklava manages to provide a strong cinnamon component, with a flaky crust and a dense filling of nuts. The recipe comes from Yanni's Greek mother, and you will see her in the deli from time to time.

## Italian

**Via Maestra 42** $$, B-L-D (3343 State St., 805/569-6522) Named for the owner's address in his hometown of Asti, Italy, this restaurant is located in an unremarkable strip mall right next to my post office, where I will pick up my royalty checks from this book. This place turns out delicious, authentic Italian food, including a wide variety of pastas and cured meats. The space is small, with a few outside seats. You can also buy Italian cheeses, meats, and gelato to take with you. Additionally, during truffle season, the restaurant imports from Italy both white and black truffles, which the public can buy and which several restaurants in town purchase. With such deftly handled food, the restaurant gets crowded, and the service is a tad slow. But it's worth the wait.

**Toma** $$$, D (tomarestaurant.com, 324 W. Cabrillo Blvd., 805/962-0777) Hands down, this is one of the best places in town. Though it bills itself as Italian, that's a rather loose descriptor; the food does incorporate Italian values, but it also expands them. For instance, the Tuna Cones are composed of diced ahi sashimi, ginger, sesame, soy, chili, and chives, all stuffed into a crisp sesame-seed cone housed in a metal candelabra (think of this as an ice-cream cone for adults). Brilliant! The braised short rib is one of the best—a baseball-sized tender rib (sans bone) is served atop whipped potatoes and red onion confit, sitting in its natural juices, and is topped with arugula and lemon oil. Love, love, love the lasagna, which is delicate and made with pesto. With so many wonderful dishes, you cannot go wrong. There's also a good cocktail program and a wine list heavy on Italian and local Italian varieties. Go!

**Trattoria Vittoria** $$, L-D (30 E. Victoria St., 805/962-5014) Lasagna is a standard dish in every Italian restaurant, but that doesn't mean it's always treated well. Here it's treated like royalty. Thin layers of house-made pasta are layered with meat and a delicate red sauce. The meat is tender and finely ground, not in chunky globs, and the red sauce is sublime—not too acidic, not too sweet. But the gnocchi due versioni is the standout: a bowl full of stunningly soft hand-made potato gnocchi with a light gorgonzola cream sauce, it achieves a delicate elegance you won't find in other gnocchi around town. This is flavorful, well-executed food in a homey, comfortable environment. It does get loud as the night wears on.

## Mexican

**Cuernavaca Taqueria** $, L-D (201 W. Carrillo St., 805/564-1414) Named for the city of Cuernavaca (meaning "place near the grove") in Mexico, this is very flavorful street food. The interior is nothing much, just a small, unadorned spot, but you're here for the food. The alambres especial is a standout dish, made with ham, cecina (salted, dried meat), bell peppers, beef, marinated pork, onions, and cheese, all grilled up together and served with a small stack of home-made corn tortillas. Single traditional tacos (not the crappy American versions) include chorizo, veggie, al pastor, and shrimp. This is terrific and authentic Mexican food, loaded with bold flavors—simple but sensational. You're welcome.

**Los Agaves** $$, L-D (los-agaves.com, 2911 De La Vina St., 805/682-2600) What started out as a standalone Mexican joint has expanded to four local spots without giving up on flavor. Yes, you can get traditional Mexican food, but hang on, Pablo, try something different. It offers a bunch of daily specials, and this is what you should go for. Consider the octopus al pesto of tender sautéed octopus with Hoja Santa pesto—made from a plant in the pepper family—and huitlacoche, also known as corn smut (I'm going to let this joke go), with a consistency similar to risotto and a mild heat and spice. The mole negro Oaxaca is grilled pork topped with roasted pasilla chili peppers, and the smooth mole is perfectly balanced, with a wonderful viscosity; it is semi-sweet and rich without being overpowering—smooth and spicy with a hint of smokiness.

## Middle Eastern

**Zaytoon** $$, D (zaytoon.com, 209 E. Canon Perdido St., 805/963-1293) An amalgamation of Middle Eastern foods, from Lebanese wine to Turkish coffee and immensely flavorful tabbouleh, hummus, and lamb, Zaytoon is a lounging spot. It has plenty of outdoor dining, with firepit tables (these need to be reserved) and belly dancers. This is not a place for a quick bite. The service can be pretty slow, most definitely on weekend nights, but it's a great overall experience, and there's nothing else like it in town.

## Pizza

**Giovanni's** $, L-D (giovannispizzasb.com, 3020 State St., 805/682-3621; 1905 Cliff Dr., 805/560-7492) Giovanni's started in 1979, and these are the original locations.

Focusing on Chicago's thick-crust style, these pizzas are packed with flavor and ingredients. I love the garlic chicken and the meat lover, which has, like, way too much meat on it. You'll also find a few vegetarian options, calzones (really just a pizza folded in half), sandwiches, and salads. The locations are junior-high-school friendly, so order for pick-up or delivery. If you like Chicago, then this Santa Barbara spot is your Wrigley Field.

**Z's Tap House** (zodos.com, 5925 Calle Real, Goleta, 805/967-0128) A restaurant inside a bowling alley with an arcade might seem like an afterthought. But Z's is located inside Zodo's Bowling and Beyond and serves up really good food, not to mention you can bowl, play arcade games, or have a beer at nearly thirty taps. The food is your basic pub food, such as pizzas, salads, and sliders, but it's flavorful, and there's more to do here than at any other restaurant in town. If you need to distract the kids, say no more.

## Seafood

You'd think there would be a ton of killer seafood places in town, but although we have lots of local fish, not many places know how to properly cook and prepare said fish. These guys do.

**Brophy Brothers** $$, L-D (brophybros.com, 119 Harbor Way, 805/966-4418) Located at the harbor, this restaurant is eternally busy serving fresh, local seafood in a hectic, loud environment. The prime seats are outside: a narrow strip of balcony crowded with people standing at the outdoor bar. But you're overlooking the boats, and a sunset dinner here with fresh seafood is awesome. The side dishes, such as salads, coleslaw, and rice, seem like afterthoughts and are kind of bland, but the entrees are exceptional. It also offers a raw oyster bar. The staff, while busy, are efficient. The restaurant doesn't take reservations, so if you arrive late you'll be in the downstairs bar waiting to be called.

**Enterprise Fish Company** $$, L-D (enterprisefishco.com, 225 State St., 805/962-3313) The interior is all hardwood floors, and there's a Disney-esque theme, not over the top but kitschy nonetheless. There's a lively bar in front, and a glassed-in kitchen, where the wood fires burn in the back. You're here for fish, so try the red snapper with basil-lime sauce topped with pine nuts. Maybe the parmesan-crusted dover sole covered with parmesan cheese and then flash grilled (so the coating becomes a crisp cheese shell) and lightly drizzled with a lemon-caper beurre blanc. Maybe the mesquite-grilled prawns. Whatever you choose, this is all-around terrific food.

**Loquita** $$$, D-Sunday Brunch (loquitasb.com, 202 State St., 805/880-3380) Spanish tapas in a town that was once owned by Spain sounds like a winner. Best known for its paella, Loquita is focused on tapas, which are small shared plates. Don't like to share? Fine, get your own. Try the chicken croquettes—deep-fried balls of chicken topped with a lemon-avocado sauce. Loquita is fun and convivial, and the energy is great; however, it's also rather loud unless you sit on the outdoor patio by the fireplace, which isn't bad either (the Spanish would definitely have approved). Specialty cocktails, such as the Montecito with local gin, absinthe, and elderflower Loquita, will make you feel like you're in Madrid . . . kinda.

### Steak

**Tee-Off** $$, D (teeoffsb.com, 3627 State St., 805/687-1616) Old school meets, well, old school. Tee-Off has been around for nearly fifty years. When you walk in, it's the kind of place where people immediately know whether you're a local. But don't worry: they like everyone. Get the prime rib; that's what Tee-Off does best. Get there early for a choice seat in the red booths, which face the bar, and pig out on way too much food, order stiff drinks, and feel the vibe of an older time. If you get there late, you'll have to wait, and we don't want you getting teed-off. Forget the fish and pastas or anything else and stick with meat. Also, bring expandable pants.

## Sushi

**Arigato Sushi** $$$, D (arigatosb.com, 1225 State St., 805/965-6074) This is excellent but pricey sushi, so bring your bucks and your patience; it's always crowded and therefore a little slow. Check out the Standing Room Only—half an avocado, baked and filled with freshwater eel and real crab. It's served in aluminum foil on a light bed of daikon shaved radishes. The gorgonzola salmon is tender pieces of salmon sashimi with red onion, dill, capers, and a gorgonzola sauce. Or consider the ginger yellow fin tuna with yuzu garlic oil, Hawaiian pink sea salt, and a dash of chives. Sure, Arigato has standard sushi rolls; non-sushi people (you know who you are) should get the Kobe beef nigiri—it's not technically sushi, but for beef lovers this is a great alternative.

**Ichiban** L-D, $$ (1812 Cliff Dr., 805/564-7653) Ichiban, a Japanese term meaning "first," has been entrenched on the Mesa for years. The interior space contains lots of wood tables, a small sushi bar, and a tatami eating area. A few Japanese pagodas and lanterns dangle from the ceiling—small accents to make it feel like Japan. Sushi rolls include the terrific 007 Roll, which is a warm

*Ichiban's 007—not shaken, not stirred.*

77

roll of shrimp and cream cheese wrapped with lightly fried salmon, then tempura fried and served with a wonderful spicy sesame sauce. There are combination meals, which include miso soup, salad, an entrée, and donburi. The restaurant also offers nightly specialty sushi, when available, served as two pieces of raw fish over a small piece of rice.

**Sushi Go Go** $, L-D (sbsushigogo.com, 119 Harbor Way, 805/962-6568) A sushi place near the water just feels right—like, the sushi is fresher, right? Well, you can't get closer to the water than the harbor and Sushi Go Go, a blink-and-you-pass-it hole in the wall that offers up some terrific sushi. A handful of tables are outside, where you can people watch, and trust me, they'll watch your food too, so be on your guard. The reasonably priced rolls are pretty typical, and you'll find chicken teriyaki and noodle dishes for those who don't like sushi. What you won't find anywhere else is my favorite—the Jalapeño Bomb—a jalapeño pepper filled with cream cheese and tuna, tempura fried, and topped with eel sauce. Yep, it's the bomb!

### Thai

**Meun Fan Thai Cafe** $$, L-D (meunfanthaicafe.com, 1819 Cliff Dr., 805/882-9244) These guys make no apologies for their very flavorful and spicy foods, served in their spot on the Mesa. Spice and heat are used liberally, so let your server know if you need a restrained version of your meal—after all, you don't want kung-pow! Try the pineapple fried rice with a bit of curry; drunken noodles with deftly prepared pan-fried noodles; or the Nam salad, made with mint, ginger, red onions, and peanuts on top of rice and lettuce, served with a healthy dash of lime juice. There is a terrific selection here. The service is well meaning but a little slow; however, the flavorful food is worth the wait.

**Tap Thai** $$, L-D (tapthaicuisine.com, 3130 State St., 805/682-1114) I've been eating this food for years; it's a staple in my house. The best things are the curries, and I don't care what you put it on, though the salmon is my favorite. You'll also find drunken noodles, various fried-rice offerings, and tofu dishes cooked so they taste like something. For an appetizer, get the corn cakes.

### Vegetarian and Vegan

**ah juice** $, L-D (ahjuice.com, 432 E. Haley, 805/698-5443) It's called pressed juice. It's not pressed for time, just juice. Certainly there is a trend toward this kind of juice, which we used to call fresh squeezed or just plain natural, but whatever the name it is pure juice, with nothing added, and is 100 percent organic, the majority of the fruits and veggies coming from local farms. The shop also offers a mushroom extract to add to your juice, but a word of caution: Drink this and you'll get invited to all the parties because you're such a fungi! Organic coffee is also available, as is a limited café menu (eggs and sandwiches), which is all organic as well.

**Backyard Bowls** $, B-L (backyardbowls.com, 3849 State St. at La Cumbre Plaza, 805/569-0011) You'll find a lot of these places in Hawaii, where the owners used to surf. Here the bowls are bigger and the prices smaller. The main focus is on the acai berry, a small purple berry from the palm tree in Brazil, which contains antioxidants and other nutritional things. This berry is then blended with fruits or vegetables and used as a smooth base in a bowl topped with fruit, granola, and other things. The berry bowl is the best, a harmonious blend of acai, bananas, strawberries, and apple juice topped with granola, honey, bananas, strawberries, and goji berries. You'll also find carrot and ginger smoothies, quinoa bowls, and the excellent peanut-butter smoothie.

## Wines, Brews, and Spirits

Not all wine tasting is done surrounded by vineyards. The Urban Wine Trail (urbanwinetrailsb.com) means you

*You'll have barrels of fun in wine country.*

can sample some of the county's best wines while never seeing a vine. Most of the tasting rooms are near lower State Street, known as the Funk Zone, a block from the beach, where you can walk to seventeen of them. There are others, all part of the trail, but that will require a little driving.

On average, tasting fees per person are $10 for five wines, but you'll see $15 and even $20 price tags on some tastings. Most places have multiple tasting lists: a standard list and a reserve list. Share a glass if you want. Do keep hydrated (with water, not more wine) and get some food, but do not drive around. Hire a taxi, a wine-tasting service, a limo, some kid with a bike, it doesn't matter—just don't drink and drive. The beauty of the wineries located downtown in the Funk Zone is that you can stumble, er, walk to most of them. Many places will waive the tasting fee if you buy something, so always ask.

**Captain Fatty's** (captainfattys.com, 6483 Calle Real, Suite D, Goleta) No, it's not the best name for a brewery, but Captain Fatty's brews some really cool, local small-batch beers. It's located in Goleta and not really near anything. The small tasting room is in an industrial park, but the brews it turns out are anything but commonplace. The staff

will fill your growler with rich and robust IPAs like Vortex, the really good tangerine brew, milk stout, or my favorite, a coffee porter. Bring the kids and the dogs (neither gets beer) and visit this convivial place.

**Corks N' Crowns** (corksandcrowns.com, 32 Anacapa St., 805/845-8600) These guys differ from most winery tasting rooms for two reasons: every month the selection of wines and beers changes; it is neither a winery nor a brewery, and therefore the selections come from all over, not just locally. Thursday evenings are for home-made flatbread pizzas and wine-pairing parties. Sunday afternoons feature sparkling wine and cupcake pairings created by Sugarcat Studio, the winner of *Cupcake Wars* on the Food Network. You can choose from five different flights of wine, including an international flight, the diamond flight of ninety-three-point and higher rated wines, and the pinot noir flight, among others. The craft beer flight features four different styles of brews, so there's something for everyone.

**Cutler's Artisan Spirits** (cutlersartisan.com, 137 Anacapa St., 805/845-4040) This place is located in our trendy Funk Zone, a scant two blocks from the beach, so now you can add vodka, gin, and whiskey to the wine and beer mix. Cutler's distills these and a few other spirits (the Apple Pie Liqueur literally tastes like apple pie, but with a kick), and many places in town use them in their cocktail programs. You can taste them here, but current law prohibits sales on the premises, meaning you have to buy a bottle some-where else—how's that for random, archaic laws that serve no purpose? Regardless, avail yourself of the only distillery in the city.

**Figueroa Mountain Brewing Co.** (figmtnbrew.com, 137 Anacapa St., 805/694-2252) This brewery only started in 2010 but has come on strong and built not only a very loyal following but also a small empire. And yes, the beers are that good. The brewery is best known for Lizard's Mouth (an IPA) and Hoppy Poppy (can you guess?), but all the beers are terrific. This location in the Funk Zone is two blocks from the beach, but the brewery has other locations in Santa Maria, Buellton, and Los Olivos, all located in the Santa Maria Valley. A visit to one of the taprooms is a must.

**Grassini Family Vineyards** (grassinifamilyvineyards.com, 24 El Paseo, 805/897-3366) If you ever thought the words cabernet sauvignon and Santa Barbara were mutually exclusive, well, those days are over. The Happy Canyon region is the single best spot to grow traditional Bordeaux varieties, and Grassini does a magnificent job with its cabernet sauvignons and sauvignon blancs. The tasting room is located downtown (there's no tasting room in Happy Canyon), and you will be amazed that this kind of quality of these varieties can be made here. The tasting room also offers special pairings (by reservation only) of local chocolates and an artisanal cheese plate.

**Hollister Brewing Company** (hollisterbrewco.com, 6980 Marketplace Dr., Goleta, 805/968-2810) These beer dudes make more than two dozen beers. For starters, the restaurant makes good food, such as duck-fat fries, pizzas, pasta, and beef. Its twelve TVs mean that guys can get a beer and watch the game (my wife is from Pittsburgh, so we watch the Steelers here). It offers sample packs—six small glasses if you don't know what to try—or you can get a pint of ale, stout, or a seasonal brew. It's an upscale brewpub doing it right.

**Kunin Wines** (kuninwines.com, 28 Anacapa St., 805/963-9633) Seth Kunin was a surfer, which doesn't have much to do with wine. He styled his wines after France's Rhone Valley varieties, such as syrah, roussanne, and viognier. There are others, to be sure: zinfandel and a really great chenin blanc (a woefully underappreciated grape), as well. The tasting room, within sight of the beach, is a small space, which looks like it was decorated with nothing but Ikea furniture. It can get crowded on summer days, and for good reason: his wines are smooth and very drinkable; the whites show best.

## Straight Up Talk About Sideways

The 2004 Oscar-winning film *Sideways* was of paramount importance to us here in Santa Barbara. Yes, many businesses saw a 30 percent jump in revenue, and it still hangs on, fourteen years later. If you are so inclined, you can visit many of the actual locations where the movie was filmed. In 2014 I covered the ten-year anniversary of the film here in Santa Barbara for *The Hollywood Reporter*, and the force is still strong.

You can find maps specific to the locations.

*Me, star Paul Giamatti, and director Alexander Payne*
*at the tenth-anniversary party*

## Antiques and Old Stuff

**Antique Center Mall** (antiquecentermall.com, 4434 Hollister Ave., 805/967-5700) A collection of twenty vendors provides everything from outdoor garden furniture and statuary to silver tea sets, mid-century modern furnishings, vintage clothing, some estate-sale pieces, and everything in between. Prices are reasonable (yes, I've bought several things here), and there's everything from the quirky (a giant white painted horse) to the mundane. It's worth a look.

**Old Town Antiques** (5186 Hollister Ave., Goleta, 805/967-2528) Located inside a shopping center, Old Town Antiques has been around for years and provides a really nice selection of vintage and retro items, offbeat stuff (a Lego head?), and customary things, such as kitchen dishes and whatnot. There's quite a bit of furniture, decorative arts, and the like. It's small but well worth a visit, as the quality is excellent.

**Unity Shoppe** (unityshoppe.org, 1219 State St., 805/965-4122) This thrift shop is an institution in town. For more than a hundred years it has been raising money for low-income families, seniors, and children. As you walk in you'll see lots of clothes, kitchen items, and jewelry, but what you don't see behind the doors is the massive facility that is the workhorse for Unity, a warehouse where food is laid out like a grocery store to help families feel more normal. A staff of fifteen, along with about 1,700 volunteers, help distribute $2 million worth of goods annually. So stop in, donate, and help others out.

## Books and the Printed Realm

**The Book Den** (bookden.com, 15 E. Anapamu St., 805/962-3321) The Den is one of those places that smells a little musty, like my grandmother's house used to. That's understandable, because this bookstore has been at it since 1933. Floor-to-ceiling shelves are packed with books, and a rolling ladder is needed to reach the top shelves. Boxes are stacked askew on top of those. If you've ever seen the TV show *Hoarders*, yeah, it's kinda like that. There is a large selection of used, out-of-print, and antiquarian books, but there is a great selection of new books, as well. The Den claims to have 1.4 million titles at its disposal, most of which simply cannot be housed in the small space. This is an old-school bookstore, and it's great to browse.

**Chaucer's Bookstore** (chaucersbooks.com, 3321 State St., in Loreto Plaza, 805/682-6787) Chaucer's opened its doors in 1974 and has become the premier independent bookstore in Santa Barbara. Everyone who can read knows Chaucer's. Why even Geoffrey Chaucer himself would buy books here, you know, if he hadn't died in 1400. There are monthly book signings from local, regional, and occasionally national authors, which means the store keeps a busy schedule. This book should be on the shelf in the travel section. If not, please raise a stink.

## Clothes and Accessories

**Tienda Ho** (tiendaho.com, 1105 State St., 805/962-3643) This is an eclectic collection of Balinese, Moroccan, and Indian fashions and furnishings, still going strong after twenty years. It's like you walked into a movie set on steroids—there's even an indoor waterfall near the dressing rooms. Colorful scarves, wraps, and skirts are just part of this collection of loose-fitting and free-flowing clothing. The upstairs is mainly furniture, cool and funky stuff better suited to a Disney theme park, but it's fun just to wander in here.

## Specialty

**Chicken Little** (chickenlittlekids.com, 1236 State St., 805/962-7771) Everything for the little ones is housed in this local thirty-six-year-old store, including toys and gifts, strollers, carriers, and backpacks, as well as sippy cups for the kids (adult sippy cups are available at the nearby bar). So, if you need to entertain the little one or need something you forgot to pack, they'll have it.

**Church of Skatan** (26 E. Gutierrez St., 805/899-1586) The Church is the only skate and board shop in town. There's a large selection of boards, trucks, shoes, clothing, and advice from the skate crowd, all housed in the old Second Baptist Church (we have no idea what happened to the first church). The original hardwood floors and stained-glass windows are the same ones parishioners once saw. To some, skateboarding is a religion already. Here, there is proof of it.

**Healthy Pet** (healthypetsb.com, 3018 State St., 805/687-2804) Because more than 90 percent of people with cats or dogs feel their pet is part of their family, and because many people travel with their pets, you might need this store while you're in town. If you don't travel with a pet and you stop by, you might be bored. The shop carries tons of healthy food options, mainly for cats and dogs, as well as toys and pet accessories to keep Fido and Fluffy distracted so you can go out and drink. Owner Rene Roberts has operated this store for a decade. I buy food for Toby and Jasper here. And my cats, Toby and Jasper, rule the world.

*Toby, left, and Jasper, lying on this manuscript—very healthy pets*

**Paseo Nuevo Mall** (paseonuevoshopping.com, 651 Paseo Nuevo, 805/963-7147) This uber-Spanish outdoor mall makes shopping fun, whether you buy anything or not. Sadly, there aren't too many local stores here, but the brick pathways meander along, with vines climbing the white walls, fountains dispensing water, colorful Mexican tiles, and the general feel of a casual afternoon in Spain. This place took its cues, and its name, from what came before it, El Paseo (listed below). So the "new" mall is a new take. There are occasional concerts and performances in the center portion, as well as a movie theatre.

**El Paseo** (downtownsb.org/go/el-paseo-of-santa-barbara, 812 State St., 805/965-1616) El Paseo started outdoor shopping. Though the complex has lost its great tenants and there's little reason anymore to wander inside the true paseo, it's still a beautiful reminder of what Santa Barbara shopping was originally envisioned to be like. Built in 1924, it was the first of its kind in the state. The meandering walkways passing through arched doorways into courtyards with wrought-iron railings and vine-covered walls give you the feel of walking through a small village. It's absolutely beautiful and is patterned after the paseos, "passageways," of Spain.

**Random** (1224 State St., 805/966-3257) You've got to love a weird store literally packed with odd, random things you never thought you needed. Stuffed with wing nuts, bolts of fabric, totem poles, comic books, strange art, one-offs, and anything that has no purpose but you'd buy it anyhow— well, you're in Random. It buys closed-out merchandise, which varies constantly, and the place looks like the worst college dorm room you can imagine. But chances are good you'll walk out with something in hand, even if you don't know what it is.

**Stay**

Santa Barbara is expensive, period. Regardless of the time of year, the weather, and even economic downturns, people come here and pay for the privilege of hanging out. Be prepared to spend cash, and don't expect many deals. Having said that, many places offer AAA discounts, various packages, and car-free discounts—meaning you arrive on Amtrak (it's a train, in case you don't know), sans car. Always ask what specials, packages, and discounts any property is offering; you might just be surprised.

## I'm on a Budget

**Harbor House Inn** (harborhouseinn.com, 104 Bath St., 805/962-9745) This is a great little property a half block from the water. They'll loan you beach towels, chairs, and umbrellas for lounging at West Beach. The seventeen rooms and studios are surprisingly well appointed, with a more home-like feel than most hotels, and they have a respectable number of furnishings you'd find in someone's house. The property itself is a little older, but the owners have done a great job of keeping it up. DVD rentals are at the front, but why the hell are you watching movies? Get outside! Best of all, you won't break the bank; the value here is one of the best in town.

**Hotel Santa Barbara** (hotelsantabarbara.com, 533 State St., 805/957-9300) If your goal is to walk outside your hotel room and be on Santa Barbara's main street, well, this is it, right where the action is—Santa Barbara action, that is. The seventy-five rooms are nicely appointed and comfortable, if a tad small for the standard rooms. There's no on-site gym, but the hotel offers a package with a local gym that you would need to drive to . . . oh, the irony. The building is an older property, so if you need hip and modern this isn't it, but this is ideal for a car-free stay in town.

**Mason Beach Inn** (masonbeachinn.com, 324 W. Mason St., 805/962-3203) This is a pretty simple white-washed hotel with forty-five rooms, and standard hotel furnishings; it won't impress *Architectural Digest*. But it's clean, close to the beach, and less expensive than most other properties around. If nothing fancy is your goal, something quick and easy for an overnight, this is a fine spot to access the beach and downtown while saving some cash. It offers a heated outdoor pool and hot tub.

**Presidio Motel** (presidiosb.com, 1620 State St., 805/963-1355) Located at mid-State Street, this is a very cool motel. The rooms are minimalist, but every room has unique decor created by UCSB students, such as abstract stars or a girl holding a parasol as she walks a tightrope above the gaping jaws of an alligator (sure, you'll sleep fine after seeing this). You're not in the thick of things, but you can still easily access many activities by walking a little farther. The motel also has complimentary beach cruisers so you can explore on two wheels, and an upstairs sun deck from which to watch the happenings on State. The young owners are dedicated to making the motel a must stop for those who want something different. It's a little bit of fun retro.

**Santa Barbara Auto Camp** (sbautocamp.com, 2717 De La Vina, 888/405-7553) An auto camp might sound like a drive-in kind of thing. It's actually four Airstream trailers you can rent for that nostalgic vibe, and there's nothing else like it in Santa Barbara. Three of the gleaming steel Airstreams are vintage 1959s, and the other is an '84. They are clean, sleek, retro . . . and small. They sit on a major street, actually in front of a trailer park, so you need to know that—they aren't located overlooking the water in some pristine park. They have tiny yards (two chairs' worth), but this quirky urban locale will be ideal for some of you.

## Life Is Pretty Good

**Agave Inn** (agaveinnsb.com, 3222 State St., 805/687-6009) This inn interprets the Spanish theme a little differently. Spanish movie posters and brightly colored throws, as well as various brightly painted walls, are the accents that set this place apart. It's like a bit of modern pop was tossed into each room. All rooms have iPod docks, and some rooms have kitchens. The inn is directly across from a small park and near Loreto Plaza, a small shopping center with a grocery store and restaurants. The thirteen-room inn is a delightful spot—very cool, hip, and simple.

**Brisas del Mar** (sbhotels.com, 223 Castillo St., 805/966-2219) Family owned and run, this place is located just two blocks from the beach. About half of the rooms are suites with full kitchens, making this thirty-one-room hotel great for a longer getaway for those who want to cook on vacation. Though the exterior is Mediterranean, the interiors have knotty pine furnishings and soft tones, a kind of design disconnect. The hotel also has covered parking, which is unusual. It has a DVD collection of more than eight hundred movies, wireless Internet, an exercise room, continental breakfast, and a gracious staff.

**Hotel Indigo** (indigosantabarbara.com, 121 State St., 805/966-6586) Hip and cool with a European sensibility, this is a refurbished hotel originally built in 1912. The forty-one rooms are smaller but nicely appointed. Murals on the walls reflect the history of the area, and photos from local photographers and, in a cool partnership, rotating art from the Contemporary Arts Forum hang about the place. There's a mini fitness room (and I do mean mini, as in like two machines) and small courtyards, and the hotel allows pets, which you can walk a block down to the beach. Drawbacks? The train tracks are right next to you, and you have to pay for parking.

**Spanish Garden Inn** (spanishgardeninn.com, 915 Garden St., 805/564-4700) These twenty-three rooms are so unknown that most locals don't even know where this place is. Tucked off State Street, this Spanish-style full-service hotel aims for stellar service while keeping a low profile. All rooms are beautifully appointed and have either balconies or patios facing a central courtyard. The inn has high-end linens, French press coffee makers, and generous bathrooms, some with soaking tubs. It's an easy three-block walk to the action, but you'll love returning to the luxurious beds and large showers. It's something of a secret (don't tell anyone), so many celebrities stay here because it's so low key.

**The Upham** (uphamhotel.com, 1404 De La Vina St., 805/962-0058) It's probably something of a privilege that the Upham can call itself the oldest continuously operating hotel in all of Santa Barbara. It opened its doors under the name the Lincoln House in 1871—you know, just after the Civil War. The property includes seven buildings, though it feels much more intimate, and is predominately centered around a garden courtyard. There are smaller rooms, ideal for a busy weekend when you're just flopping, or larger rooms with fireplaces and more space for the stay-in weekend. The Upham has an attached restaurant, Louie's (pretty good), and you're within walking distance to State Street, though you're a cab ride to the beach. The degree of antiquity of the rooms varies; some are from the 1800s, the 1920s, and so forth.

## I Just Won the Lottery

**The Ritz-Carlton Bacara** (ritzcarlton.com, 8301 Hollister Ave., Goleta, 805/968-0100) An Andalusian-style village of suites and rooms just steps from the crashing surf—what's not to like? Perched on eighty acres of prime Pacific coast shoreline, it's exclusive and expensive, but that's the point. The rooms are large, with sliding doors to views of the ocean. It's all five-star here, and with multiple restaurants, a spa, and even a little shopping on site. You may not spend a million bucks (maybe half a mil), but you will definitely feel like it. The downside is that it's not really near anything, well, except the beach. You'll need your car or a taxi to get to downtown Santa Barbara, a fifteen-minute drive. Or, since you're so fancy-pants for staying here, hire a car.

**Belmond El Encanto** (belmond.com, 800 Alvarado Place, 805/845-5800) Santa Barbara basks in its reputation as the America Riviera (a self-described title), and the Belmond El Encanto Hotel—perched on a low mountain rising above the sparkling Pacific Ocean, overlooking the red-tile roofs of downtown Santa Barbara—is a classic retreat worthy of its location. This historic property, built in 1918, has a storied lineage, including visits by FDR and Clark Gable. It is set up as cottages dotting the landscape, and brick pathways guide you to your spacious room; up-to-date amenities belie the classic Craftsman sensibility. The outdoor zero-edge salt-water pool affords views straight out to the Pacific Ocean and the Channel Islands framed by mature eucalyptus trees. The pool is kept between eighty and eighty-six degrees (based on warmer and colder weather), and the hotel offers poolside service with a special menu and cocktails, complimentary sunglasses cleaning, and Evian cooling spray. The openness of the pool and its unfettered views both out and up to the skies is one of the remarkable charms of the El Encanto. Do know, however, that the property is removed from downtown, and you will need a car to access anything you want to do.

**Canary Hotel** (canarysantabarbara.com, 31 W. Carrillo, 805/884-0300) This hotel's best selling point, other than its dead-center location, is its rooftop deck with a pool and fireplace. On summer nights you can lounge here for hours under the stars with some excellent views. The interiors are smartly designed, with a Moroccan feel with Spanish undertones and hardwood floors. It's kind of like a modern-day Casablanca. This hotel has the best access to State Street and all that it offers. The ninety-seven rooms and suites are a little small for the money, but they are beautifully done. The Canary offers the only rooftop pool in all of Santa Barbara County. The pool is heated to eighty-two degrees and includes underwater lighting and Mediterranean-inspired tiles. You have views to the Channel Islands and as far south as Ventura, not to mention Santa Barbara's red-tiled roofs and the Los Padres mountains. The pool's Wellness Station features chilled towels scented with lavender from the garden, local farmers-market fruits, and a variety of complimentary sunscreen and aloe. Poolside yoga is offered on Saturday mornings.

## Planes, Trains, and Automobiles

### *Planes*

**Santa Barbara Airport** (flysba.com, 500 James Fowler Rd., Goleta, 805/683-4011) Santa Barbara is a small town, so naturally we have a small airport, but it is cute! Currently (it keeps changing) it serves regional flights from six destinations and three airlines. The drive from Los Angeles is two hours,

but the flight is twenty-five minutes; from San Francisco the drive is six hours, but the flight is thirty-five minutes. Do the math. Inside the airport are a restaurant, gift shop (with some of my other books, thank you), and coffee shop—that's it. However, we do have our very own airport therapy dog named Loki, so if you're feeling stressed, pet him. Do not pet your neighbor.

*Loki, the airport therapy dog*

### Trains

**Amtrak** (amtrak.com, 209 State St., 805/963-1015) The train pulls right into Santa Barbara, a block from the beach, and lets you out in the historic, but unimpressive, 1905 depot right on State Street. If you make Santa Barbara a day trip, this is a great option. Greyhound buses arrive here too.

### Automobiles

Santa Barbara is accessed by state Highway 101 from the north and south. If you drive from LA it's ninety miles. No, there are no secret routes. If the 101 is clogged, you're pretty much SOL. The only other way to access Santa Barbara via long, winding, and weird drives is from state Highway 192 from Ojai, and Highway 154 (a.k.a. the San Marcos Pass) from the north, but that still requires you to take the 101 partway. You can get to Santa Barbara from LA via the Santa Barbara Air Bus (sbairbus.com, 805/964-7759), which runs about $45 one way and is pretty good considering that the traffic will be your driver's problem, not yours.

## Local Media

**The Santa Barbara News-Press** (newspress.com) is the controversial daily paper. Much of the news is aggregated from other sources, but there are some local stories.

**The Santa Barbara Independent** (independent.com) publishes every Thursday and is free and located everywhere. It has good entertainment listings, including shows, concerts, theater productions, and films.

**Noozhawk** (noozhawk.com) is an online publication filled with local stories and information.

**KEYT** (keyt.com) is the main TV station broadcasting from Santa Barbara (channel three here in town). You can get the latest mildly professional news.

**Channel 17** is the local community access TV show, with way too much coverage of city hall meetings and various boards and commissions. But it also offers some local programming.

## Local Resources

A great resource for bike trails, walking paths, trains, taxis, water excursions, and all manner of transportation is **Santa Barbara Car Free** (santabarbaracarfree.org), which offers downloadable maps and ways to experience Santa Barbara while reducing your carbon footprint.

Check out the **Axxess Book** (sbaxxess.com) if you visit regularly. This local discount book has raised hundreds of thousands of dollars for local schools, and you'll get two-for-one offers and discounts on wine and beer tastings, restaurants, shopping, and entertainment from more than five hundred local vendors. I have one, and so should you. You'll be surprised at the savings, not to mention you will be tempted to try something new!

**Santa Barbara Chamber of Commerce Visitors Center** (sbchamber.org, 1 Garden St., 805/965-3021) This tiny stone building is located directly across from the beach and offers discounted tickets to many restaurants and sights in town. However, just because tickets are discounted doesn't mean you need to go. It has a small selection of books about the area—and this book had better be there!

**State Street Trolley** (sbmtd.gov) For just fifty cents, you can ride the length of the waterfront, or the length of State Street. Two electric shuttle routes serve downtown (State Street) and the waterfront (Cabrillo Boulevard) daily, every half hour. Children under forty-five inches ride free, and a free transfer is available between the downtown shuttle and the waterfront shuttle; just ask your driver.

## Parking

Laid out like a grid, Santa Barbara is easy to navigate—well, at least the downtown core. Of particular note is that State Street, the defining street, travels from the oceanfront in a northwest direction and makes a ninety-degree bend (known as Upper State Street) to then run east and west. Eventually State Street turns into Hollister, and by then you're entering Goleta. But all things fan out from State Street, and most directions are given in relationship to State. There are plenty of parking lots along State St., and the beach and typically the first 75 minutes of any City parking lot is free! For rates, real-time parking info and more, check out santabarbaraca.gov/gov/depts/pw/dtp/

### Street Names

As local historian Neal Graffy writes, "Unlike other towns whose streets bore the unimaginative A-Z, numbers, trees, or names of presidents, they (the town founders) gave names to our streets that portrayed the geography and botany of our town, honored the Chumash, early settlers, governors, and showed a distinct sense of humor and, in some cases, delightful sarcasm." To that end, well, here ya go.

- Most streets have unique names, and there's little possibility of confusing them. But, of course, there's always something. Three specific streets will cause a problem here in town: Castillo, Carrillo, and Cabrillo. Here's what you need to know. Cabrillo (think of the B as in beach) runs the length of the waterfront. Carrillo (think of the R as running right through town) bisects State Street. And Castillo (think of the S) parallels State Street. With that in mind, it should be easier getting around. If not, call a cab.

- If you find yourself on Salsipuedes Street, it is allegedly an old Indian term (it's actually Spanish and is three words mashed together) meaning something like "get out while you can"—a reference to the flooding of the flatlands during the rainy season.

- Indio Muerto means "dead Indian" because, allegedly, a dead Indian was found near here. Didn't see that coming, did you?
- Many streets were named after former governors (I see why politics is so intoxicating), including Arrellaga, Sola, Victoria, and Figueroa.
- Anapamu is an Indian term meaning something like "the rising place." Some locals call it Animal Poo, but that's not funny.
- Yanonali Street was named after a Chumash Indian chief.
- Lou Dillon Lane was not named for a guy named Lou but rather a horse, a trotter, who broke a trotting record in 1903. Lou the horse is buried near here. If there is some guy named Lou Dillon out there, uh, sorry about that.

# CARPINTERIA, MONTECITO, AND SUMMERLAND

South of Santa Barbara and north of the Ventura County line are the small, intimate communities of Carpinteria, Montecito, and Summerland. Often overlooked, they nonetheless provide the area with small-town charm and offer some cool stuff that big sister Santa Barbara doesn't. Carpinteria is its own city, whereas Montecito and Summerland are unincorporated areas within the county, even though they seem remote from the county as a whole. And, frankly, they like it like this.

## Hello, My Name Is . . .

**Carpinteria** used to be home to fields of lima beans, walnut orchards, and oil derricks, oh my. The Chumash people who lived here used the naturally occurring sepes (oil and gas coming up from the ocean—this is why sometimes the beach smells like tar) and asphalt to seal abalone shells to be used as bowls and to seal their seaworthy boats, called tomols. When Cabrillo passed by here in 1542 on his ship, he decided to call the area San Roque, after, we think, the name of a saint. But when Gaspar de Portola's expedition was in town in 1769, the abundant tools the industrious Chumash used looked like a carpenter's shop, hence La Carpinteria. Now it's small-town America, and a walk down Linden Avenue, the main drag, is like a walk back in time; it's also a three-block walk to the beach.

**Montecito** has long been associated with wealth, which is why I don't live there. It certainly is one of the priciest zip codes in California, and with residents like Oprah Winfrey and many Hollywood folks, the allure of mammoth estates continues. It's a quiet enclave, hidden behind huge hedges, fences, gates—anything to keep people away. Tucked into the foothills, its main artery is Coast Village Road, a small, trendy shopping district, known locally as CVR or the Lower Village. Literally a mile and a half north is the small, unassuming Upper Village, which is, in Montecito terms, a world away.

**Summerland**, by contrast, hugs the coast, and pretty much the entire community looks out to the ocean. Even the mobile-home park has better views than most people who live around here. It was nicknamed "Spookville" because of the spiritualists who once lived in the area, and many people driving north from LA took back roads around Summerland to bypass the "weirdos" and to avoid the harsh stench of oil from the beaches and oil platforms in the ocean. Today Summerland is a languid stop, a one-street wonder with a handful of restaurants and stores.

## The Mystery of History

Summerland, the smallest community, has the biggest story. A dude named Henry Williams planned to farm on his 1,100-acre parcel, but he ran into financial difficulties. Stroke of luck: the Southern Pacific Railroad was laying tracks north from Los Angeles and would cross his ranch near the beach. Williams decided to build a town next to the rails and sell lots. In 1887 the first train passed through the ranch on its way to Santa Barbara, and in 1889 Williams and the early settlers dedicated their town, calling it Summerland. See, Williams was a spiritualist and believed in a physical place called Summerland, where our spirit beings wait, having left the Earth, until their next incarnations back here on Earth. Sort of like a spiritual rest stop . . . but cleaner. For a few years the spiritualists continued to come, and many built homes and started businesses. Land was donated for the construction of a temple where they could gather socially and for séances, where mediums contacted the spirits of their relatives and friends who had passed over. All was well until the discovery of oil, which brought new, non-spiritualist people to the tiny town who were anxious to make their own fortunes. Hotels and rooming houses were built, and saloons were popular gathering spots, to the dismay of the spiritualists. Residents in Montecito hated the look and smell of their small neighbor to the east, and some oil wells and oil facilities were actually sabotaged, including those of J. Paul Getty, who joined the drilling community for a short time. The oil boom lasted only about ten years before supplies began to dwindle, but drilling did continue until the 1920s.

In **Montecito** it was a much different story. Wealthy Easterners came here with lots of money and found the foothills to be ideal for setting up large estates, away from rowdy Santa Barbara and silly Summerland. Those estates still exist today. Prior to that, the first settlers were farmers, planting fruit and nut trees, cultivating wine grapes, and raising cattle. And even before that, Montecito was considered a potential site to build the mission.

**Carpinteria**, though home to several tribes of Chumash, was mainly a salt marsh, which still exists today. Sure, the Spanish and then the Mexicans worked the land; it was rich in oil and even became a center of asphalt mining. Because the land wasn't near Santa Barbara, it was easy to use much of it for farming, cattle, and orchards—it is a pretty wide valley, and land was inexpensive. It wasn't until around 1870, when wealthy Montecito residents began to buy up more inland property, that anyone really took note of the area.

## Weird and Trivial . . . But True!

ⓘ In 1968, local McDonald's franchise owner Herb Peterson from Montecito "invented" the Egg McMuffin. Really? That had to be invented?

ⓘ You may like strolling the beaches of Summerland, but in the 1890s they were literally covered with oil derricks.

ⓘ The largest grapevine on record, according to the *Guinness Book of World Records*, is known as the La Vina Grande and was originally planted around 1840 in Carpinteria. It grew so large it was actually a polling location for voters in 1850. Its circumference measured nine feet, nine inches, and bunches of grapes weighed in at nine to ten pounds. It was more than nine feet tall and covered half an acre. It eventually died around 1924.

*La Vina Grande with lots of happy people*

ⓘ Not to be outdone, the "Parra Grande," another mammoth vine, took root in Montecito. According to historic accounts, the circumference was nine feet, seven inches. Its annual harvest was around ten tons of fruit, and the vine provided shade for dances, meetings, elections, and funerals. A bonehead named Dr. James Ord cut it down and sent it to the Centennial Exposition in Philadelphia in 1876. That makes us whine.

ⓘ The very first offshore oil drilling, certainly in the Northern Hemisphere and some claim the world, was constructed off the beach at Summerland. Drill, baby, drill.

ⓘ The Ortega Adobe, a historic two-story adobe, is the site of a cold-case murder mystery. On Christmas Eve, 1881, an Italian winemaker named Giovanni Trabucco was murdered here for his gold. The gold was never found, and the murderers were never caught.

## Arts and Galleries

**The Gallery Montecito** (thegallerymontecito.com, 1277 Coast Village Rd., Montecito, 805/969-1180) A small, airy space, this gallery features local art as well as works by internationally known artists. It shows both traditional and modern influences, including painting and photography. Its exhibitions rotate and often have a philanthropic aspect, raising money for various nonprofits, which is a pretty cool idea.

## Festivals and Events

**Avocado Festival** (avofest.com) This festival is held each October in Carpinteria, and you'll be green with envy if you miss it. Santa Barbara has tons of groves of avocado trees, sadly fenced off so you can't pick them. About seventy thousand people flock to worship this tree fruit during the three-day festival, which is free and open to the public. Forty different bands perform, and there are arts and crafts and, yes, a guacamole contest (which I judged one year). All manner of foods are made with avocados, be they brownies, ice cream, or beer. Because the region is the third-largest producer of

*"Best Dressed Avocados" at the Avocado Festival*

avocados, it only makes sense we'd celebrate it. Our first avocado orchard was planted in 1895 in Montecito.

## Health and Wellness

**The Spa at the Four Seasons** (fourseasons.com/santabarbara/spa, 1260 Channel Dr., Montecito, 805/969-2261) The spa is as comfortable and relaxing as its beachside location. Beach cruisers for the family are available for rent, and there are eleven treatment rooms and an on-site trainer upon request. The gym portion of the spa is outfitted with Technogym treadmills, allowing you to upload any exercise apps you already have on your smartphone. They are also equipped with air-conditioning units and touch screens so guests can exercise in specific places filmed on location, kind of like your own reality show. There are free weights, and you can also schedule private yoga or Pilates classes. For a pre- or post-spa respite, the garden by the entrance, with its three-tiered fountain and views to the beach, is perfect. Begin your spa treatment in the relaxation lounge, a second-floor quiet room that offers dried fruits and nuts, a fireplace in the corner, and ocean views visible from plush, comfortable chairs. The treatment rooms, with clean maple flooring, are designed for singles, though there are couples' suites. Four treatment rooms are master suites with an outdoor patio and views to the ocean; a Jacuzzi tub and two massage tables and champagne can be incorporated into any service. It's no surprise that you can get most anything you want, from massages (including stone work, Swedish, and maternity massage) to facials. One of the most popular treatments is the Grape De Vine scrub, using grape seeds straight from Santa Barbara wine country. Oh, and the spa offers in-room dog massage so Fido can feel frisky, too.

## Museums

### Carpinteria Valley Museum of History

(carpinteriahistoricalmuseum.org, 956 Maple Ave., 805/684-3112, free) No more than a thirty-minute visit is needed here, but it's so small-town, cute, and interesting that it's worth the stop. Sure, Santa Barbara gets all the attention, but the history of this area, once one of the largest producers of asphalt—yes, I said asphalt—is worth considering. There are only a few rooms here, showcasing period furniture and farming history, including some rusty farming equipment.

## Nightlife

**Alcazar Theatre** (thealcazar.org, 4916 Carpinteria Ave., Carpinteria, 805/684-6380) Okay, if you need hip clubs you head to Santa Barbara, but this old theater, built in 1928, does offer live music, movie nights, karaoke, and occasional evening lectures. Oh, and yes, it offers live theater. It's a small venue for a small town, maintaining the vibe of small-town America.

## Outdoor Activities

### AIR

The closest airborne activity you can find here is deep breathing followed by a walk on the beach. In Montecito, there's plenty of hot air, but that's another story.

### EARTH

#### Hike

**Carpinteria Bluffs and Seal Rookery** This is less of a hike and more of an easy stroll on soft dirt paths. The bluffs are a great beach excursion across eucalyptus-studded groves heading to the water. It's only a mile out and a mile back, but this coastal walk is perfect for any age and fitness level; in fact, the elevation gain is like two feet. The scent of chaparral meets you as you pull into the parking lot, with low grasses and shrubs in front of you. There is also access down to the beach; however, part of the beach is closed December 1 through May 31 during birthing and nursing season for the harbor seals who seem to think mating in public is just fine (showoffs). They are noisy but fun to watch. Located right off the freeway, this is immensely easy to access, and it gets you to views of both the ocean and the mountains and to the water's edge while still feeling like you're in a preserve. That feeling is briefly interrupted by the train tracks, but as long as there are no actual trains in your way, it's all good. You might see whales and dolphins, and certainly plenty of sea birds (not on the train, on the hike). To get there, exit on Bailard Avenue from Highway 101 and head to the ocean. There's a small parking lot right in front of you.

#### Polo

**Santa Barbara Polo & Racquet Club** (sbpolo.com, 3375 Foothill Rd., Carpinteria, 805/684-6683) Forget tennis; you can do that anywhere. But polo is quite cool and has

*Santa Barbara horsey polo*

been played in Santa Barbara since 1911. Nothing says fun like grown men chasing a little ball on horseback with a stick. The polo club is the third oldest in the US, and you can attend a tournament. It's $10, and the days are limited (because this *is* a club, dear boy), but you really should go if you've never been. The horses are amazing, and you can get pretty close to the action here. Ladies, wear a hat and good shoes for the divot stomp. From the top of the grandstand you can see the ocean, and the mountains bookend the other view. Not a bad way to spend an afternoon.

## FIRE

Beach fires are permitted at **Carpinteria State Beach**, but only in fire rings. So grab a bottle of local wine, some wood, and a few s'mores, and you're in business.

## WATER

**Butterfly Beach** (Channel Drive across from the Four Seasons Biltmore, Montecito) The narrow Butterfly Beach is accessed by a handful of steps. Many people come here to catch a glimpse of a celebrity from nearby Montecito, but chances are that won't happen. To find the beach, take

Highway 101 to Olive Mill Road in Montecito. At the stop sign, turn toward the ocean (you know, away from the mountains) and follow the road a quarter mile along the coast. Butterfly Beach is on your left. Parking is limited and will be packed on most weekends and often on weekdays. Bring your lunch, water, and sunscreen, because there are no public facilities at this beach. Dogs roam freely here. At high tide you have no access to the sand, but you can walk along the road.

**Carpinteria State Beach** (5361 Sixth St., Carpinteria, 805/684-2811) This beach has the self-proclaimed title of "World's Safest Beach." Whether that's an understatement or not, this beautiful, wide, flat beach is definitely a favorite among locals and tourists. You'll have everything you need: there are plenty of campgrounds, picnic tables, outdoor showers, RV hookups, and telephones, and it's a short walk to Linden Avenue, where you'll find restaurants, shops, and a grocery store. Parts of the campgrounds are tree lined, but you're right next to the train tracks, so if you camp you might get woken up unexpectedly.

## Sites: Historic

**Casa del Herrero** (casadelherrero.com, 1387 E. Valley Rd., 805/565-5653, $25, reservations mandatory) Spanish for "house of the blacksmith," this place seems like just another Spanish façade in a town overrun with thousands of Spanish-style houses. But from the moment you enter the lobby and see the Tibetan eighteenth-century wood ceiling, you know you're in another world. Designed by owner George Fox Steedman and prolific Santa Barbara architect, George Washington Smith, it was completed in 1925. The estate, essentially unchanged from its original state, is Spanish Colonial Revival architecture at its best. The house is on the National Register of Historic Places and is a National Historic Landmark, and for good reason. The amount of detail is overwhelming, from tile work and hand-carved door surrounds to furniture from Europe. In fact, Steedman altered the house to fit the doors and windows he purchased while traveling abroad. Though it is ornate and elaborate, furnished with authentic Spanish antiques, and awash in architectural details, the home still has an amazing sense of proportion. Steedman also commissioned local artist Channing Peake to add a Western flair to some of the original art. The tour includes the gardens, as well. All in all, a really cool place to visit.

**Lotusland** (lotusland.org, 695 Ashley Rd., 805/969-9990, $35, reservations mandatory) This lush garden is thirty-seven acres of the most well-manicured and lovingly tended gardens you will probably ever see. It was last owned by Madame Ganna Walska, a Polish opera singer in the 1920s and quite the drama queen; she routinely arranged her vast collections of plants into bold color schemes and unusual shapes. Her vast collection of lovers, well, that's a different story. For more than four decades she tinkered with her gardens. But the estate was made for this. The first owner had a commercial nursery on the land in the 1880s. After Walska's death in 1984, the Lotusland estate—so named because of the lotus flowers on the property—became a nonprofit. It is one thing to visit a botanical garden, but it's another to wander through a magnificent wonderland of plants, trees, and gardens. From the moonscape barrenness of the cactus gardens to the topiary garden, the serene Japanese garden, the olive allee, and the formal English-style gardens, Lotusland is that rare stop where you feel you could stay forever. In fact, one of the staff gardeners has been there for more than thirty years. It is truly an awe-inspiring place. It can get brisk, as many parts are so heavily wooded that they don't get much sun. The wide walking paths easily accommodate wheelchairs.

**Our Lady of Mount Carmel Catholic Church** (olmc-montecito.com, 1300 E. Valley Rd., 805/969-6868, free) Deviating from the mission feel of most churches in the area, this baby is going for a more pueblo revival idiom (I love the word idiom). This working Catholic church was built in 1936, upgraded from a ramshackle working parish started in 1856. The unique architec-

*Our Lady, who art a church . . .*

tural style was patterned after Pueblo Indian missions built in New Mexico and Arizona. Typifying the handiwork of the Indians are the uneven window openings and irregularly plastered walls, and you might think you've had too much communion wine. No, it's made to look that way. The rustic feel of the church separates it from anything else in the county as a unique house of worship.

## Coffee and Other Stimulants

**Four Seasons Biltmore Afternoon Tea** (fourseasons.com/santabarbara, 1260 Channel Dr., Montecito, 805/969-2261) Afternoon tea (sometimes called "high tea," but that's not correct) has been offered at the Four Seasons Biltmore since 1987. The full afternoon tea includes two courses: a selection of finger sandwiches and then an

*Afternoon tea, Montecito style*

assortment of pastries, scones, cheesecake, crumpets, and chocolate-covered strawberries. There are twelve teas to choose from, including standards such as Earl Grey and unique options such as peppermint herbal and Japanese sencha. If you want to get a light buzz, upgrade to the glass of sherry, or Kir Royale. Sit by the fireplace or sit outside, across from Butterfly Beach, watch the languid ocean, and act like a proper British subject.

**Red Kettle Coffee** (redkettlecoffee.com, 2275 Ortega Hill Rd., Summerland, 805/565-1900) Just as cute as a red kettle, this homey spot offers locally roasted coffee as well as smoothies, teas, and a few baked goods. There are a handful of gift items, as well, and even a small library where you can take a book or leave a book. There is a small bar with a few stools, so most people make their way to the back patio, where you will find Dobkin, a wooden gnome, holding his own red cup (we assume full of wood chips).

## Restaurants and Food

**Bree'osh Cafe** $, B-L (breeosh.com, 1150 Coast Village Rd., Montecito, 805/570-9151) As sophisticated as Montecito is, there was no French bakery anywhere! (Okay, breathe.) Finally it happened when husband and wife team Pierre and Nelly (he from Brittany, she from Bordeaux) opened this teeny tiny place in 2015, which has become unquestionably popular. Aside from the two tables inside (no fun because the line forms around you and people stare at your food . . . creepy), the outside tables are the place to be. Must try: the ridiculously light and airy quiche, proper French pastries, and a *tres magnifique* Croque Madame, along with sandwiches and a decent coffee menu.

**Clementine's Steak House** $$, D (4631 Carpinteria Ave., Carpinteria, 805/684-5119) Walking into Clementine's old-timey eatery, you immediately comprehend that this is a throwback to an era that is nearly extinct. Muzak plays over the speakers, the older clientele talk quietly amongst themselves, and the decor is 1960s country farmhouse. Burgundy tablecloths are contrasted with pink scalloped napkins. All entrees come with a crudité plate and house-baked bread, soup, salad, and pie. It's a tremendous amount of food, and nearly everyone leaves with leftovers. It also takes time, so if you're in a rush, this low-key place won't be for you. With steaks, seafood, pasta, and chicken, it's traditional and homey. And, like I said, you get pie.

**Honor Bar** $$, L-D (1255 Coast Village Rd., Montecito, 805/969-6964) With its corner location and bright yellow umbrellas, the Honor Bar beckons travelers on Coast Village Road. Housed in a Spanish colonial building, the interior is quite small and is taken up with a center bar facing an open kitchen, so seating goes quickly and wait times can be long. A few booths hug the walls. The menu is limited, but solid with its choices. For a starter, consider the herbaceous trout dip, or the deviled eggs with pickle relish and scallions. For mains, the classic French dip with an earthy au jus is satisfying, as are the fluffy spinach omelet and the seared ahi with shiitake ponzu sauce. But it is the burgers that are the signature dish—fresh ground beef and cheddar, topped with coleslaw. A small wine list provides predominately local wines, as well as a smattering from Europe and Napa. Cocktails are also available, and a small selection of beers. Dogs hang out at the outdoor patio.

**Plow & Angel** $$$, D (sanysidroranch.com, 900 San Ysidro Ln., Montecito, 805/565-1700) Located at the trendy San Ysidro Ranch, this restaurant is all beautiful, large hewn-stone blocks. The space is intimate, with a fireplace, a handful of tables, round amber-hued stained-glass windows, and a six-seat bar. Long-standing signature dishes include the macaroni and cheese and Colorado lamb sliders. Monday through Wednesday are considered locals' nights, and the restaurant offers a comprehensive meal of soup or salad, entrée, and dessert for a set price (but I'm guessing you're not a local). The seafood paella is also one of the best bets. It's a charming, small space for a good but pricey meal, but you have to valet your car.

**Sakana** $$, L-D (1046 Coast Village Rd., Montecito, 805/565-2014) Tucked into the farthest corner of the forgettable Vons shopping center, Sakana seems to enjoy being under the radar, except for the fact that devoted sushi lovers flood this place, and for good reason. Highly creative, thoughtfully prepared, and beautifully orchestrated sushi and rolls are what it does best. Stick with things like the pink bear roll of panko-breaded and fried salmon, crab, cream cheese, and cilantro, with blood-orange vinaigrette drizzled on top; the Sakana roll—fried halibut, cucumber, and avocado topped with seared tuna; or the straightforward yuzu pepper kanpachi—kawari sushi of yellowtail with yuzu pepper, habañero sauce, and truffle soy sauce. It's pricey, so be aware of that.

**Sly's** $$, L-D (slysonline.com, 686 Linden Ave., Carpinteria, 805/684-6666) Sly's is classic American fare, such as beautifully tender steaks, fresh local abalone, and pastas. Chef James Sly knows how to cook (he helmed Lucky's in Montecito for years), so look for him behind the grill (he looks like Santa Claus). The interior is high-end retro, with gorgeous wood tones, exposed brickwork, and white tablecloths. And the food is nearly perfect, as long as James is in the kitchen. It's pricey here, but very dependable. For brunch, get the abalone and eggs.

**Tydes at the Coral Casino** $$$$, L-D (coralcasinoclub. com, 1281 Channel Dr., Montecito, 805/565-8285) The Coral Casino is a private club, so getting access isn't easy. Either you know a member or you're staying at the Four Seasons. And this, my friends, is one of the single best places for dinner anywhere in Santa Barbara. Built in 1937, it's always been the exclusive spot for people other than me (though I'm here several times a year). Yes, the food is spectacular, and if you get a table on the second-floor balcony as the ocean crashes below you and the sun sets over Butterfly Beach, you'll think you might be in heaven. Yes, the food and drink are pricey, but the renovated 1930s retro feel is spot on. The aquarium bar allows you to watch fish swim underneath your drinks.

**Zookers** $$, L-D (zookersrestaurant.com, 5404 Carpin-teria Ave., Carpinteria, 805/684-8893) For fifteen years Zookers has been one of Carpinteria's best restaurants. Perhaps oddly, it presents nothing unique food-wise in this cool, orchid-laden restaurant, but what it does, it does very well, be that pasta chicken saltimbocca, sesame-crusted ahi, or turkey-mushroom meatloaf. This is a local favorite, with rotating local art on the walls and indoor and outdoor seating. Though Carpinteria is not a culinary landmark, at least Zookers does a very admirable job with fresh, clean food.

## Chocolates and Sweets

**Chocolats du CaliBressan** (chococalibressan.com, 4193 Carpinteria Ave., Carpinteria, 805/684-6900) If a chocolate shop is run by a French chocolatier, you're pretty much guaranteed to get fab bonbons, truffles, single-origin chocolates—anything to satisfy your sweet tooth. When you walk in, you're hit with a heady aroma of all things chocolate; the treats are made on the premises in the back. The marzipan lips and the salted caramel Buddhas are the top sellers. The shop offers tours once a month; the cost is $20, which includes a glass of champagne. Two words: Must go. There's a second shop in Santa Barbara, which is retail only, at 1100 State Street (805/568-1313).

**Pierre Lafond Montecito Market** (montecitoshopping.com, 516 San Ysidro Rd., Montecito, 805/565-1503) Located in the Upper Village, this market has an astounding selection of chocolates sold by the piece, some local and others from literally across the globe, including Vietnam. Most are in bar form. A while back I did a wine and chocolate tasting here, in part because of its vast selection. The market doesn't make its own, but you'll traverse the planet here. Additionally, the deli sells wine cake by the slice and loaf. It's incredible. From a forty-year-old PTA recipe book, it's stunningly moist, and there's nothing like it anywhere.

**Robitaille's Candies** (robitaillescandies.com, 900 Linden Ave., Carpinteria, 805/684-9340) This spot is an institution, having been making and selling chocolates for more than four decades. Though it carries some prepackaged items it doesn't make on-site, it is best known for its original thin mints, little discs of multi-colored mints that fly off the shelves like tiny Frisbees, and which were served at President Reagan's inauguration in 1985 and George H.W.

Bush's inauguration in 1989. It also has a big selection of sugar-free candies (oh, the irony . . . and the shame).

## Wines, Brews, and Spirits

**Corktree Cellars** (corktreecellars.com, 910 Linden Ave., Carpinteria, 805/684-1400) Stocking a diverse range of wine and beer (some local, most not), Corktree Cellars has also expanded into food, beyond the original tapas idea. If you find a wine or beer you like, take it home to meet your mother from the retail section! Otherwise, cozy up in the small bistro with a glass of wine or a bottle or brew and enjoy the night.

**Island Brewing Company** (islandbrewingcompany.com, 5049 Sixth St., Carpinteria, 805/745-8272) Brewed a block from the beach, the Blonde is basic but crisp and clean. The IPA is lighter on the hops but still has hoppy notes. The Jubilee is more mocha, with slightly hoppy back-notes. The Holiday is that cleaner brew with bubble-gum notes, while the stout is dense and rich. You sit just near the train tracks and look out across a grassy field to the ocean, with Santa Cruz Island taunting you in the distance. The point of a brewery like this is fresh, clean brews, and this does the job nicely, thank you.

**Liquor & Wine Grotto** (montecitovino.com, 1271 Coast Village Rd., Montecito, 805/969-5939) This is one of the best-stocked liquor stores around, with lots of high-end and hard-to-find wines and liquor. It's tight quarters in here, but if you have a hankering for something other than local wines, you'll get a terrific selection here. This isn't a liquor store that sells beef jerky, salty snacks, and knockoff booze; this is the real deal, with beverages you won't find even in your own favorite liquor store.

## Antiques and Old Stuff

**Antico II Antiques** (2280 Lillie Ave., Summerland, 805/565-4899) This shop has beautiful museum-quality antiques, a lot of French and Asian furniture, accent pieces, tables, and unusual items, such as a nineteenth-century Chinese wedding bed and a birdhouse built as a replica of the Kremlin. Prices here are not shy, but you'll also not find many things like this.

**Brostrom's** (539 San Ysidro Rd., Montecito, 805/565-0039) Located in the Upper Village, Allen Brostrom's shop has been around since 1982, with a focus on Asian decorative arts, antiques, and vintage pieces. There are truly some beautiful things here—lacquer-painted chests and bureaus, vases, and really unique items, such as a scepter I found here once. It's not all Asian-themed, mind you, but if the Orient orients you, you'll be happy here.

**Summerland Antique Collective** (summerlandantiquecollective.com, 2192 Ortega Hill Rd., Summerland, 805/565-3189) This is the oldest collective in the area, having survived for more than thirty years. About 45,000 square feet of everything you can imagine—mid-century modern, jewelry, retro, artwork, and garden furnishings—is all here under one roof, and a few are under mine. There are deals, but you need to search for them, and there's a lot to look through.

## Books and the Printed Realm

**Tecolote Book Shop** (tecolotebookshop.com, 1470 E. Valley Rd., Montecito, 805/969-4977) This bookstore originally opened its Dutch doors in 1925 (if you don't know what Dutch doors are, look it up). These days the carpet and beautiful wood bookcases that line the 1,300-square-foot space make it feel more library than bookstore. Supported by very loyal locals, it's the oldest bookstore in the county, and that's saying something about small independent book-stores . . . that, or the good people of Montecito like to have a few friends over when they read.

## Specialty

**The Sacred Space** (thesacredspace.com, 2594 Lillie Ave., Summerland, 805/565-5535) Room after room of chubby little Buddhas fill this funky, meandering space along with a ton of Asian-themed books, antiques, and decor. Oh, yes, there are other deities to be had for a fee—all manner of sacred things, including prosperity elephants. For those who are extremely curious—and more spiritual than I am—there's a beautiful little bench in the very back that the Dalai Lama sat on when he gave a lecture at UCSB. Outside is a series of intimate spaces surrounded by a bamboo wall mixed with old carved doors. Soft water fea-tures call to you with languid running water, and there is a general sense of wellbeing here.

## Life Is Pretty Good

**Inn on Summer Hill** (innonsummerhill.com, 2520 Lillie Ave., Summerland, 805/969-9998) This is a Craftsman-style sixteen-room place built specifically as an inn. It's not a reconstituted house, though it might look like one. And? Well, that's important, because the rooms are spacious and, yes, you can see the ocean. Each room has a gas fire-place (concrete logs, my friends) and Jacuzzi tub. The inn has a dedicated chef who makes pretty impressive break-fasts, and because this is a B&B it's included in the price. You will hear the faint rumbling of Highway 101, but you may not care.

**Montecito Inn** (montecitoinn.com, 1295 Coast Village Rd., 805/969-7854) In the late 1920s, movie star Charlie Chaplin wanted a getaway from his hectic Hollywood schedule, so he gathered some investors and built this inn—more as a getaway for himself and his friends than as an actual inn. These days it's still as charming as it was intended to be. The sixty-one rooms are small, the halls even smaller, but that's how life was back then, full of small people. This is a wonderful historic property, and vintage Chaplin posters line the walls. There's also a collection of Chaplin's DVDs to watch in your room. It's only two blocks to the beach, and you are situated on Coast Village Road (locals call it CVR), the tony Montecito shopping district.

## I Just Won the Lottery

**Four Seasons Biltmore** (fourseasons.com, 1260 Channel Dr., 805/969-2261) This is classic Santa Barbara. The prime property sits just above Butterfly Beach in Montecito, with killer views to the Channel Islands. This has long held its ground as one of the best places to stay. It is laid out like a small Spanish village, and the lush landscaping, including ferns and bougainvillea, creates an almost tropical feel—but, you know, without the humidity. You can walk to shops and restaurants on Coast Village Road or drive into downtown Santa Barbara. The hotel faces Montecito's Butterfly Beach and is just steps from the ocean. The three outdoor pools are tucked behind the hotel amidst two thousand species of plants, flanked by lush vegetation, such as Australian tree ferns and Kentia palm trees. The main pool, which is hand tiled, is heated to eighty-six degrees and is outfitted with an underwater sound system. There are also two smaller pools, one filled with mineral water drawn from the property itself and heated to 104 degrees. The other small pool, which is ideal for kids, uses non-well water and is heated to ninety-four degrees.

During the summer there is poolside service, including treats from Santa Barbara's oldest ice-cream shop, McConnell's. The hotel also offers complimentary sunscreen and aloe, sunglasses cleaning, and children's toys.

**San Ysidro Ranch** (sanysidroranch.com, 900 San Ysidro Ln., 805/565-1700) The Ranch has forty-one individually and lushly appointed rustic cottages and suites tucked neatly into the mountains. Despite exceptional ocean views from the hideaway, you're not near much of anything—but that's the point. Rooms range from small and intimate to the 1,300-square-foot Kennedy Cottage where JFK and Jackie honeymooned in 1953. The Ranch has two restaurants, so if you decide to stay in and wander the mountain retreat, at least you can return to some food; otherwise, get your car from the valet.

## Planes, Trains, and Automobiles

### Planes

**Santa Barbara Airport** (flysba.com, 500 James Fowler Rd., 805/683-4011) Ours is a small airport that currently (it keeps changing) serves regional flights from six destinations and three airlines. You can get to Carpinteria from LA via the Santa Barbara Air Bus (santabarbaraairbus.com, 805/964-7759), which runs about $45 one-way and is pretty good.

### Trains

**Amtrak** (amtrak.com, 209 State St., 805/963-1015) pulls right into Santa Barbara and lets you out in the historic 1905 depot right on State Street, one block from the beach. Greyhound arrives here too.

## Automobiles

Carpinteria and Montecito are accessed by state Highway 101 from the north and south. If you drive from LA, it's ninety miles, so plan on two hours by car. If you're driving from San Francisco, it's a six-hour drive. And that's pretty much it. There are no secret routes. If the 101 is clogged, you're pretty much SOL.

## Local Resources

**The Montecito Journal** (montecitojournal.net) is the weekly paper for all things Montecito, including a gossip page because so many gossipy things happen here. Celebrity sightings are routine.

**Carpinteria Magazine** is a quarterly magazine with more in-depth stories on the area.

**Coastal View News** (coastalview.com) is another weekly paper, mainly for Carpinteria, but it includes a listing of current happenings. These are free, and you can find them most anywhere.

# SOLVANG

## Hello, My Name Is . . .

I've never been to Denmark, but Solvang is pretty much Denmark on steroids, and this colorful and charming village-like town is unlike any other town in the area, or the state for that matter; it's a great escape from the tedious mall architecture that dominates much of America. You'll notice storks displayed above many of the stores in town; they're a traditional symbol of good luck. Solvang draws nearly two million visitors each year, and you'll still hear the muted strains of Danish spoken on occasion (there's even one local bakery where the "Danish mafia" hang out and talk to each other in their native tongue, but without guns or names like Scarface).

During peak summer times and holidays, Solvang can be congested, with people clogging the brick sidewalks, riding rented surreys through the streets, and loitering in front of the bakeries and chocolate shops, and it feels uncharacteristic of a small town. It's best to visit during the off-season, when the simple joys of meandering past the lovely shops are evident. It's at its best in the fall and early spring, when the hills are verdant green and the trees in town are beautiful.

*Solvang, meaning sunny fields, is a must stop when visiting Santa Barbara.*

139

## The Mystery of History

Solvang was the brain-child of three Danish guys. Originally the town looked like other towns of the day—a Spanish theme punctuated by Western stores. Post WWII saw the emergence of a vision to create the Solvang we see today. Long before the-matic towns or city centers were in vogue, Solvang agreed on a unifying design theme, and that is part of the allure. Solvang, which

*Solvang's founding fathers—these are wood carvings, not the real guys*

means "sunny fields," was first settled by Danes who migrated to these sunny fields in 1910. The town fathers bought about nine thousand acres from the Santa Ynez Mission and set up shop, literally, and the town was cre-ated in 1911. The goal was to create a home away from home, and the first buildings were the Lutheran church and a Danish folk school, which still stands as the Bit O' Denmark restaurant. Today Solvang is still ripe with its Scandinavian heritage, along with a new, modern sensibil-ity. Yes, the theme park atmosphere is not lacking in kitsch. Some people mistakenly believe that Solvang should look like Copenhagen, when in fact the town was a farming settlement. Yes, it does look like older farming villages from back in the day.

## Weird and Trivial . . . But True!

ⓘ You'll see carved storks above many stores. Why? In Denmark it's considered a sign of good luck. And they don't poop.

140

ⓘ More royalty have visited Solvang than any other town on the Central Coast: in 1939 Danish Crown Prince Frederik and Princess Ingrid visited; in 1960 it was Princess Margrethe of Denmark, who returned in 1976 as queen of Denmark; in 2011 it was Henrik, the prince consort. Well la-dee-da.

ⓘ Solvang was featured in an episode of *The Simpsons*, which included several mentions of "Danish butter cookies."

ⓘ Hans Christian Andersen (who epitomizes the Danes and Solvang) was the most widely traveled Danish writer of his day in the mid-1830s. His best-known tales are "The Emperor's New Clothes," "The Little Mermaid," "The Princess and the Pea," "The Red Shoes," and "Thumbelina." Andersen wrote more than 160 fairy tales, which have been translated into more than a hundred languages. What have you done today?

## Arts and Galleries

**Pavlov Art Gallery** (pavlovgallery.com, 1608 Copenhagen Dr., 805/686-1080) Husband and wife team Chris and Iris Pavlov helm this gallery, where you might salivate over the art, but you won't get any food. They are local residents— he paints and uses mixed media; she does photography. The gallery has rotating exhibits of other artists' ceramics and jewelry. Much of Chris's work reflects the outdoors, honoring his childhood in Macedonia.

## Festivals and Events

**Danish Days** (solvangusa.com) Held the third weekend in September, Danish Days is a big draw. Started in 1936, it features clog-wearing Danes dancing in the streets wearing traditional Danish dress. Pastries and coffee are everywhere, and there's even an *æbleskiver* eating contest . . . uh, yeah. It's Solvang's annual salute to its cultural heritage, and local women dress in traditional skirts, aprons, and caps, despite the heat of the season. The men too wear their clogs and traditional outfits. The event is also referred to as Æbleskiver Days on occa-

*Doing the Danish Days dance. Photo courtesy Solvang CVB*

sion, and it has long been a tradition for locals to set up their *æbleskiver* pans in the streets and serve them to people (not the pans, they keep those). If you want a colorful immersion into Danish culture, you can't do better than this.

**Taste of Solvang** (solvangusa.com) This event has been in existence for two decades, and it keeps growing and becoming more sophisticated each year; it now lasts a week. Held in March, it starts with a dessert reception, and considering the pastry and sweets history of the Danes, that's enough right there. Following that is the walking smorgasbord that features roughly forty stops in town, where you pop in and sample whatever they might be serving, from Danish meatballs and red cabbage to Italian sausages to Danish pastries like the classic æbleskiver. If you get there early, you can make a pretty good meal of the whole thing while wandering the town. In the evening is the wine and beer walk (closer to the wine and beer stumble as the night progresses) where wine and beer tasting rooms pour their vintages into your souvenir glass. This is one of the most popular events and does sell out.

**Solvang Century** (bikescor.com, 800/548-4447) This is the best-known cycling race in the Valley. Well, technically it's not a race but rather a fundraiser, but you still can't help but compete. Organizers have added a half-century (fifty-mile) race to accommodate riders who prefer the shorter distances (that would be me), but there is still some pretty serious elevation gain of about two thousand feet, making this a challenging course. The money raised benefits heart-related diseases because the founder of the event used cycling to promote health after his own heart surgery. It's been more than forty years, and people still flock to this very popular event.

## Health and Wellness

**Haven Day Spa** (hadstenhouse.com, 1450 Mission Dr., 805/688-3210) This spa is hidden behind antique Asian doors. Inside, the spa reveals quiet, soft color tones and offers a mix of facials, massages, body wraps, and even tuning fork therapy, which utilizes strategically placed tuning forks to bring harmony and balance back to the nervous system, muscles, and organs. It also does couples' massages, so if you need a partner and you're paying, I might be available. The staff here is knowledgeable and ready to accommodate.

## Museums

**Elverhøj Museum** (elverhoj.org, 1624 Elverhoy Way, 805/686-1211, $4) This museum is just so way cool. The Elverhøj (meaning "elves' hill" and also not a Tolkien reference) will help you understand Solvang and why this dinky town carries such important historical and cultural significance. There are lots of old photos and traditional crafts. Of particular note is the typical Danish kitchen, hand painted in green with stenciled flowers and with pine floors, countertops, and tables; it gives an idea of how creatively the

*Inside the Elverhøj*

Danes decorated their homes, no doubt in an effort to brighten bleak winters. Those winters brightened considerably after the Danes arrived in Solvang. The museum also features exhibits of traditional folk art from Denmark, such as paper cutting and lace making, which is clearly evident throughout town. There are displays of wood clogs and the rustic tools used in the process, and the museum offers rotating exhibits throughout the year focused on the Valley. It would be easy to dismiss the museum as just a novelty, but clearly the passion of the original settlers and their determination to come to America and continue their way of life is something we can all learn from. That is ultimately the beauty of America: the ability to share with everyone different cultures and traditions.

**Hans Christian Andersen Museum** (bookloftsolvang.com, 1680 Mission Dr., 805/688-2052, free) This museum has a few artifacts of Mr. Andersen, including a bronze bust (a copy of which is in the park on Mission Drive); first editions of his books from the 1830s, some in Danish and some in English; photographs; and a timeline chronicling his life and work and his impact on literature. It's easy to overlook Andersen as simply a writer of fairy tales, but Andersen also wrote novels, plays, and other works and was quite highly regarded in his time. This museum pays homage to a Dane who made his mark on the world. Even a short visit will enlighten you to his prolific work.

**Solvang Vintage Motorcycle Museum** (motosolvang.com, 320 Alisal Rd., 805/686-9522, $10, weekends only) This is truly a unique and interesting stop. Ninety-five motorcycles, both vintage and new, are on display on this self-guided tour—basically a big-ass room with cool-ass cycles. Each bike has a description, and some are downright beautiful because they have been polished and perfectly restored. There are bikes from the 1930s and 1940s, the earliest from 1903, and some are so cool you'll want to strap on a helmet and ride. This is a private collection that includes Ducati, Crocker, Matchless, Nimbus, and many others.

## Outdoor Activities

### EARTH

**River Course at the Alisal** (rivercourse.com, 150 Alisal Rd., 805/688-6042) Golf at this eighteen-hole, par-seventy-two course that was featured in the *Sideways* movie. It's a beautiful course on the banks of the Santa Ynez River, punctuated with magnificent oak trees. This challenging course features four lakes, open fairways, tricky hazards, and large, undulating greens accented by native sycamore trees (because "alisal" means "grove of sycamores"). Elevated tees reveal some vistas and occasional vineyards, so bring your best game and your camera. Greens fees are under $75, which is pretty impressive.

**Hans Christian Andersen Park** (500 Chalk Hill Rd.) At fifteen acres, this is the largest park in the area. You enter through a castle gate, and you're amidst pine and oak trees. Then you come to the skate park, which has cavern-ous half pipes and is actually well designed, though more bikers use it than boarders. A small wooden playground sits behind the skate park for the younger ones. If you continue driving through the well-groomed park, you'll come to another playground with tall chute slides embed-ded in the sand. There are plenty of trees and picnic tables to relax at and have a picnic. If you drive all the way to the end, four tennis courts reside right next to a beauti-ful, gnarled old oak tree. There are restroom facilities and drinking fountains.

**Sunny Fields Park** (900 Alamo Pintado, 805/688-7529) This is a pint-sized version of Solvang . . . kind of. A Viking ship, swings, slides, and monkey bars are intertwined with a gingerbread house and a faux windmill. Spindly trees offer some shade during the summer, but not much. Located on the outskirts of Solvang, it's away from the bustle. There are drinking fountains and restrooms, plenty of parking, and a large, grassy ballfield to burn off the pastries you've prob-ably just consumed.

## Sites: Historic

**Mission Santa Ines** (missionsantaines.org, 1760 Mission Dr., 805/688-4815, $5) This site has overcome natural disasters, political turmoil, and financial hardships and remains a working church to this day. It is named after Saint Agnes (Ines), hence Santa Ines. The town, however, is spelled Santa Ynez, which is the Spanish spelling. The mission, established in 1804, was designed to be a stopping point between the missions of Santa Barbara and La Purisima in Lompoc. It was devastated by the earthquake of 1812 and then rebuilt; what it visible today is not original, with the exception of part of the arch toward the south end of the property. The Chumash population was reported to be close to a thousand at the peak of the Mission period. After

Mexican Independence from Spain in 1821, secularization caused the departure of the Spanish missionaries, and most of the Chumash, and the decline of the mission itself until it was rescued and restored. Mission Santa Ines historical records show that between 1804 and 1850 there were 1,631 baptisms of Native Americans. During that same period there were 1,632 deaths. Coincidence? I think not.

The interior church is long, tall, and narrow, simply decorated with hand-painted motifs and without much architectural detail. Of note is the large collection of about five hundred church vestments (really special clothing) held here, dating from the fifteenth century to the early 1700s. No, you can't play dress up. Outside near the stations of the cross at the south end of the property, you'll find expansive views to the valley below, which used to have orchards for the mission. Few people know about the back entrance through a parking lot at Mission and Alisal roads in Solvang. Behind the public restrooms, a brick walkway leads to the back of the mission grounds.

## Sites: Not Exactly Historic

**OstrichLand** (ostrichlandusa.com, 610 E. Highway 246, 805/686-9696, $5) Made popular by the film *Sideways*, this bird farm is two miles from Solvang off Highway 101.

At first glance it seems somewhat prehistoric—massive birds in the distance wander through the shrubs, reminiscent of *Jurassic Park* but without the tiny arms. They usually keep their distance and only approach when there is food to be had. Should you decide to feed them, you need

*Ready, set, eat!*

147

to hold the metal food plate firmly in your hand; they do not eat calmly—no charm school training here. These hefty birds attack the plate like it's their last meal on death row. A loose grip and you've wasted $4—and your kids might be in tears. Aside from feeding them, you can shop for ostrich eggs, ostrich jerky, emu eggs, ostrich feathers, and the like.

## Bars

**Randy's Taproom** (1525 Mission Dr., 805/686-9456) Owner Randy Ophaug used to be in the antiques business and then decided to open a taproom and game room. The result is lots of board games, a pool table, darts, antique gaming tables, and other odd antiques, all in a haphazard former clothing store that no one bothered to renovate. The taproom offers live music, brews on tap, and wines by the glass, and it's open late in the notoriously we-shut-early town. This place works precisely because it's not trying to be cool and hip, it just is.

**Wandering Dog Wine Bar** (wanderingdogwinebar.com, 1539 Mission Dr., 805/686-9126) This isn't really a bar— yes, I know it's in the name. It's a wine and beer spot, not a cocktail spot. This is not the place to fetch standard merlot and chardonnay; this is the place to push your palate because the bar seeks out under-the-radar wines and brews, many of which aren't local. It offers flights, as well, including sparkling wines. Thursday nights it sells cheese plates and does blind tastings, so you can improve your wine knowledge. Weekends it's open till 10 p.m., which is pretty crazy for Solvang.

## Restaurants and Food

Danish cuisine doesn't conjure up images of innovative global fare. Yes, many places in town serve traditional

Danish food, and if you've never had it it's worth a try. Like what? Well, *medisterpolse* (Danish sausage), *frikadeller* (meatballs), *rodkaal* (red cabbage, not "roadkill"), *spege-sild* (pickled herring), and the most well-known Solvang delight, *æbleskiver,* which in Denmark is served only at Christmas. Here, well, apparently every day is Christmas. You can buy them at many places, or buy the ingredients to make them at home. For those who are intrepid enough, I have the recipe, courtesy of Solvang Restaurant.

## Æbleskiver

Ingredients: 2 cups buttermilk, 2 eggs, 1/2 tsp. salt, 2 Tbsp. sugar, 2 cups flour, 2 tsp. baking powder, 1/2 tsp. baking soda, 4 Tbsp. melted butter

Firstly, get an *æbleskiver* pan, which resembles a muffin pan, if it was made to cook golf balls. Separate the eggs. Mix egg yolks and all the other ingredients together at one time and beat until smooth. Allow batter to set for 30 minutes. Beat the egg whites stiff and fold in last. Heat *æbleskiver* pan. Put 1 tsp. salad oil in each hole and fill completely with batter. Let bake until slightly crusty on bottom. Turn slightly with a knitting needle or skewer. Continue cooking, turning the ball to keep it from burning, until the knitting needle comes out clean when stuck in the center. Serve hot with powdered sugar and jelly.

**Bit o' Denmark Restaurant** $$, L-D, (bitodenmarkrestaurant. com, 473 Alisal Rd., 805/688-5426) This is the oldest restaurant in Solvang (1929) and is housed in one of the first buildings the original settlers built in 1911. If you want traditional Danish food, here ya go. Known for its traditional smorgasbord, as well as roasted duck and Monte Cristo sandwiches, it also cooks up Danish ham and pork. The extensive smorgasbord includes traditional Danish foods and an array of cold salads. The room to the left as you enter is the best, with large curved booths.

**El Rancho Market** $, L-D (elranchomarket.com, 2886 Mission Dr., 805/688-4300) This is an upscale full-service supermarket and features an old-fashioned full-service meat counter, fresh local organic produce, and a complete selection of local and international wines, champagnes, and spirits. It has very good hot and cold entrees (I love the whiskey meatballs), salads, fresh baked bread, and pies, all perfect for planning a picnic. If you want something quick and easy to eat, it has a great selection. It has some out-door seating near the entrance, and on occasion workers grill tri-tip outside.

**Hadsten House Restaurant** $$, L-D (hadstenhouse.com, 1450 Mission Dr., 805/688-3210) This restaurant entered the dining scene just a few years ago but immediately ele-vated the local culinary perspective. It is dark and moody inside, and a central fireplace creates a hip urban environ-ment—more metropolitan than rural. The short ribs have a demi-glace that will set your mind reeling, and the warm spinach salad is perfectly balanced. Go for the Hadsten burger, which is piled with everything, including an egg. It's best to make reservations, as it's a small space produc-ing some very fine food.

**Root 246** $$$, L-D (root-246.com, 420 Alisal Rd., 805/686-8681) Sleek and sophisticated, Root 246 has upped the ante on fine dining in town. It looks like it belongs in Hollywood, not in rural Solvang. But that's part of the evolution of Solvang and wine country cuisine. The menu rotates often depending on seasonal ingredients. You'll find oysters, organic mushroom flatbread, and a variety of fish and game dishes. The clientele is more the young, urban crowd, and you don't see a lot of old-school Danish residents here.

**Solvang Restaurant** $$, B-L-D (solvangrestaurant.com, 1672 Copenhagen Dr., 805/688-4645) Solvang Restaurant is well known for its æbleskiver, a round, doughy concoction topped with jam. Don't be surprised to see a line out the door; the restaurant has a take-away window just for this. This little diner also dishes up breakfasts in a quaint environment. The overhead wood beams are decorated with Danish proverbs, including "Luck stands behind the one who dares" and my personal favorite out of the twelve that are there: "The one who saves for the night, saves for the cat." OK, anyhow . . . of note, one of the booths near the back was used in the film *Sideways*, and you can sit where Miles and Jack did (there's a plaque there, so it's a cool photo op).

**Succulent Café** $$, B-L-D (succulentcafe.com, 1555 Mission Dr., 805/691-9444) Everyone wants food that's succulent, fresh, and flavorful, and with Succulent Café you'll get just that. There are both indoor and outdoor tables in a rustic environment. Weekends are popular, so there tends to be a wait. In addition to a broad menu, it has a line of its own canned goods focused on farm-to-table ingredients. Try the fried chicken and gravy biscuit, a breakfast sandwich of a buttermilk biscuit, crispy and moist fried chicken, and aged cheddar cheese, all drizzled with bacon gravy and topped with an egg. This is filling, maybe a little fattening, but oh so good. Or try the meatloaf, which continues the comfort-food theme.

**Cecco Ristorante** $$, L-D (ceccoristorante.com, 475 First St., 805/688-8880) Cecco is proud of its Italian brick pizza oven, so naturally we were curious what comes out of it. In addition to the dozen other pizzas, the Cinghiale, consisting of wild boar sausage, crispy kale, and smoked mozzarella, is a terrific thin-crust pizza. The Risotto Nero is probably the most unusual dish in the restaurant, and perhaps all of Solvang for that matter. Rice is covered with black squid ink, scallops, and a lobster brodo (broth) and highlighted with red onion and heirloom tomato.

## Chocolates and Sweets

**Ingeborg's Danish Chocolates** (ingeborgs.com, 1679 Copenhagen Dr., 805/688-5612) Ingeborg was originally from Denmark, but she moved to Solvang to escape the conflicts of World War II. She used to pass out her stick mints in front of her store to entice people to come inside. Yeah, like that's ever an issue! Her recipes live on, and her namesake store has been making traditional Danish chocolates for nearly half a century. It sources its base chocolate from the West Indies. Danish chocolate deviates from, say, Swiss chocolate in that the Danes have a slightly sweeter tooth, so even the dark chocolate isn't terribly bitter, and the cacao percentages are lower. More than seventy varieties of chocolate are available here, handmade on the premises, including the uniquely Danish flødebolle—a marshmallow crème on top of a marzipan crust, dipped in dark chocolate. It also carries hard-to-find Dutch chocolates. Or, grab a seat at one of the six red barstools and enjoy the ice cream or gelato with fresh local fruits.

## Danish Bakeries

Perhaps amusingly, the term "Danish" refers unequivocally to breakfast pastries, but they weren't perfected in Denmark; they are of Austrian origin. Who cares? In Solvang we celebrate all things Danish—and, let's be honest, no one ever asks for an "Austrian pastry." Here are the bakeries in Solvang where you can get your damn Denmark Danish.

**Mortensen's Danish Bakery** (mortensensbakery.com, 1588 Mission Dr., 805-688-8373) One of the stalwarts of the Danish bakeries in town for the past four decades, Mortensen's is open every day but Christmas. It's best to stop in for a strudel, an éclair, and a pot of tea or coffee and relax in the subdued environment. This bakery doesn't have over-the-top Danish décor—in fact, it's rather low key—but it's still good Danish and a great way to start your day. Get some butter cookies.

**Olsen's Danish Village Bakery** (olsensdanishvillagebakery. com, 1529 Mission Dr., 805/688-6314) This bakery was established in Denmark way back in 1890, though this location isn't quite that old. It's been turning out homemade breads, such as grain pumpernickel, sunflower-seed pumpernickel, and Swedish cardamom, as well as cookies and all manner of sweets, for more than three decades. Every December you'll find a giant gingerbread house here. No, I mean big, as in ten feet tall and eleven feet long! And no, you can't eat your way out of it.

**Solvang Bakery** (solvangbakery.com, 438 Alisal Rd., 805/688-4939) This bakery is a bright, open space in a blue and white shop with an eye-catching array of gingerbread houses, Danish waffles, almond butter rings, and plenty more. It has been baking in Solvang for thirty-five years. Its onion cheese bread is a signature loaf.

## Wines, Brews, and Spirits

There are twenty tasting rooms and several breweries right in downtown Solvang; others take a short drive. These won't disappoint.

**Lincourt Winery** (lincourtwines.com, 1711 Alamo Pintado Rd., 805/688-8554) This winery is named for the daughters of owner Bill Foley, Lindsay and Courtney. Another fun tidbit: the tasting room is in an authentic 1926 Sears catalogue house purchased for (ahem) like $400. Also, the wines are excellent. The pinot noir and chardonnay are the best bets here, and the wines are reasonably priced, if a tad more expensive than you might want. It also does cabernet and merlot very well, especially for an area not known for these wines.

**Presidio Winery** (presidiowinery.com, 1603 Copenhagen Dr., 805/693-8585) This is one of the few wineries in all of the Central Coast to be certified as a biodynamic winery. You'll see a small Demeter label on the back of the bottles, as this is the authoritative body that governs this farming method. Biodynamic is beyond organic and employs, ideally, a closed-loop farm system. Simply put, it's farming the best way to ensure that intrusive outside elements don't interfere with a healthy respect for the land. That aside, owner Doug Braun's wines are quite good, and his style of winemaking is more restrained than most that you'll taste in the area. Chardonnay, pinot noir, syrah, and late harvest wines are on offer at his storefront on Mission Drive, a great stopping place to begin your education about local wines and his farming methods.

**Rideau Vineyard** (rideauvineyard.com, 1562 Alamo Pintado Rd., 805/688-0717) Housed in an 1884 two-story adobe, one of the few such buildings left in all of California, this winery emphasizes Rhone varieties: syrah, viognier, roussanne, and grenache, as well as riesling, grenache blanc, and port. It has a small gift shop with some New Orleans inspired items because owner Iris Rideau originally hails from Louisiana. The winery has concerts several times each year, where you'll find gumbo and other Creole foods. It's a beautiful spot to enjoy a picnic on the lush, green back lawn. Tastings are done both inside and outside, and staff members love to give out Mardi Gras beads. I mean, no one is taking their shirt off, but you'll still get the beads.

**Rusack Vineyards** (rusackvineyards.com, 1819 Ballard Canyon Rd., 805/688-1278) A short drive is needed to get to one of the best picnic spots in the valley. Bring your lunch and pick up a bottle of the winery's sauvignon blanc, sangiovese, pinot noir, or the flagship Bordeaux wine called anacapa; you can lounge under the old oaks on the side deck. Ballard Canyon is, for the most part, a quiet canyon, and the views of the other vineyards from the outside patio are wonderful. Around Halloween the canyon is dotted with bright pumpkins, and you'll occasionally see bison roaming the hills.

## Antiques and Old Stuff

**Solvang Antiques** (solvangantiques.com, 1693 Copenhagen Dr., 805/686-2322) This spot is a high-end collection of all things with a provenance. It is home to some incredible antiques, some of which have found their way into my own home. In addition to a stellar collection of magnificent gilded antique clocks, you'll find music boxes, jewelry, watches, candlesticks, and gorgeous vintage telephones from the 1930s (I bought a cool cobalt blue one). It also has artfully restored antique furniture. The seven-thousand-square-foot showroom has more than sixty-five specialty dealers from around the globe and is like the ultimate candy store for serious antique lovers. This is an expensive place but has such diversity that any antique lover should stop in, even if you don't intend to purchase anything, just to bask in one of the finest stores along the Central Coast.

## Books and the Printed Realm

**The Book Loft** (bookloftsolvang.com, 1680 Mission Dr., 805/688-6010) This bookstore sells predominately new books, with a small section of used ones. This four-decades-old, two-story store has a vast, well-organized wall-to-wall selection of authors, including locals. The wood stairs creak as you venture upstairs to see even more books. It has the feel of an old bookstore, not sanitized with fancy shelves, and in fact these shelves were all hand made. It also has a nice selection of antiquarian books and a sizable selection of Danish, Swedish, and Norwegian authors, not to mention Danish-language books. Upstairs is the Hans Christian Andersen Museum.

## Clothes and Accessories

**Copenhagen House** (thecopenhagenhouse.com, 1660 Copenhagen Dr., 805/693-5000) All things Denmark are housed in this house (actually a former bank built in 1919), be it clothes, jewelry, kitchenware, or even furniture, including some of the top Danish designers in the world. What you can't miss is the elephant in the room. Or, rather, the eight-hundred-pound, ten-foot statue carved out of American cedar wood of the Danish mythical hero Holger Danske, the sleeping Viking who never died. The Danish owners say that this particular Holger Danske will wake up and come to the rescue if the "Danishness of Solvang ever gets in trouble." Translation? Play nice.

**Elna's Dress Shop** (elnas.com, 1673 Copenhagen Dr., 805/688-4525) I'm sure everyone thinks little Danish kids in little Danish clothes look cool, cute, and completely captivating. Well, Elna's is your stop for handmade Danish dresses and costumes. Aprons, caps, and simple, brightly colored dresses—some with beautiful lace—are off the rack, or Elna's will make one for you. It has a few Danish

*Handmade Danish dresses. What else do you need?*

pieces for young boys, as well, and yes, these are pretty damn cute. The store opened in 1942, and these are original patterns. You can't get more Solvang-Danish than this.

## Specialty

**Jule Hus** (solvangschristmashouse.com, 1580 Mission Dr., 805/688-6601) Yes, it's insanely over the top, but it's Christmas here every day. You'll find hand-carved wood, blown-glass, and traditional Scandinavian ornaments; Danish quilts, lace items, and nutcrackers—lots of nutcrackers. If Christmas makes you nauseous, don't come here. But if you need holiday cheer in, say, March, come on by. This shop has celebrated the Christmas spirit every day since 1967. That's a lot of ho ho hoing.

**Nordic Knives** (nordicknives.com, 436 First St., 805/688-3612) What's more Nordic than knives? Yes, it's a rather odd store for a mild tourist town like Solvang, but you'll find more knives than you can imagine, so cut them some slack. This store has it all, including expensive, high-end custom knives tricked out with jewels and engravings.

Sure, there are also hunting and kitchen knives, but those aren't as cool as the sleek ceremonial and show knives. The shop has been around since 1971, and the staff know their knives. If you need a simple knife, Swiss army knife, or some Japanese samurai sword, this shop has it.

## I'm on a Budget

**Solvang Gardens Lodge** (solvanggardens.com, 293 Alisal Rd., 805/688-4404) This is a twenty-four-room delight. Just on the edge of town, it feels like a small village. Each room is unique; some have marbled bathrooms or stone fireplaces. Some are decorated with a modern theme, and some have a more traditional feel, but all are very well appointed. Beautiful gardens in both the front and center of the property give you a peaceful green space. The lodge is locally owned, and the staff will do everything they can to ensure your stay is the best it can be. Not being on the main drag, it's quieter here, and you're closer to the golf course, which means a nice morning walk down to the dry riverbed. You can still smell the bakeries operating early in the morning, and it's only a few blocks to the main street.

## Life Is Pretty Good

**Hadsten House** (hadstenhouse.com, 1450 Mission Dr., 805/688-3210) This non-smoking property is one of the best places to stay in Solvang. French-style furnishings, custom mattresses, dark furniture, and ample space pull you out of the Danish mentality and into a contemporary and sophisticated setting. There's a full breakfast and a nightly wine and cheese offering, as well as a heated outdoor pool and hot tub. This is one of the closest hotels to Highway 101 and the first you come to as you enter Solvang. Set in a square horseshoe pattern, the property offers no views, except across the street to another hotel. Regardless, these are comfortable, well-appointed rooms with a European flair.

**Hotel Corque** (hotelcorque.com, 400 Alisal Rd., 800/624-5572) This hotel is a complete departure from the Danish-themed town. Hip, modern, and sophisticated, it feels like it belongs in a major city, not a rural area. But that's part of the beauty. This was originally a very Danish hotel; after an extensive renovation, it has morphed into a sleek and sophisticated hotel catering to a younger crowd. Though the one hundred rooms and seventeen suites are a tad small, there's no disliking the décor. The amenities are standard, but if you're looking for cool digs, this is it.

**Mirabelle Inn** (mirabelleinn.com, 409 First St., 805/688-1703) Run by seasoned veterans of the hospitality industry, the inn has ten medium-sized rooms. They are Victorian B&B in their feel, decorated with antiques and lace, and many have four-poster beds or even sleigh beds. Located in the heart of Solvang, the inn allows you to leave the vine-covered walls and go explore, and then return to another world.

**Wine Valley Inn** (winevalleyinn.com, 1564 Copenhagen Dr., 805/688-2111) With fifty-six rooms and six cottages, this place is larger than it looks, and the rooms are spacious. The interiors are bathed in soft tones. Some of the rooms have fireplaces, either wood burning or artificial. The inn is right downtown, so you can do without a car. I've stayed here several times, and it's a quality place to stay.

## I Just Won the Lottery

**Alisal Guest Ranch and Resort** (alisal.com, 1054 Alisal Rd., 805/688-6411) This property dates back to 1946. The seventy-three rooms at this ranch retreat are large and have a strong Western and Pueblo feel. Because this is a retreat and not a hotel proper, there are no in-room TVs, telephones, mini-bars, or room service. But you do have access to wireless Internet, tennis courts, a golf course, fishing in the lake, horseback riding, and even archery. It's glorious rustic luxury here and is secluded enough to relax you. You can walk into Solvang when you're tired of the solitude. The ranch offers a number of different packages, including a popular BBQ bootcamp where you can learn to grill the real way!

## Planes, Trains, and Automobiles

### Planes

**Santa Ynez Airport** (santaynezairport.com) is small, I mean like one runway, and it's built for private and charter aircraft. So, if you've got the money . . .

### Trains

**Amtrak** connects to the Valley via motor coach, a.k.a. a bus. The bus stop is located at 1630 Mission Drive in Solvang; however, the trains stop only in Santa Barbara and San Luis Obispo. Travel times for the coaches are approximately one hour. Every Saturday, the Clean Air Express deluxe bus service connects Santa Barbara to Solvang.

### Automobiles

Highway 246 bisects the town. Known as Mission Drive in town, the 246 connects to Highway 101, which is the primary freeway on the Central Coast, and the small but still well-traveled Route 154, which connects to Santa Barbara to the south and Highway 101 farther north. It's important to note that Solvang gets crowded on weekends, and getting in and out can be a slow proposition. All parking is *free* throughout Solvang. Six electric vehicle (EV) charging stations are located downtown.

## Local Resources

**Santa Ynez Valley News** (www.syvnews.com) covers what happens in Solvang and the surrounding areas.

**The Solvang Visitors Center** (solvangusa.com, 1639 Copenhagen Dr., 800/468-6765) is manned by locals wearing red vests. They have comprehensive information not only on Solvang but also on the entire valley.

FOXEN CANYON WINE TRAIL

FIRESTONE

CURTIS

ANDREW MURRAY

FOXEN

ZACA MESA

REDFORD THOMPSON

BYRON

RANCHO SISQUOC

COTTONWOOD

CAMBRIA

KOEHLER

# SANTA YNEZ AND THE SANTA MARIA VALLEY: SANTA BARBARA'S WINE COUNTRY

The heart of Santa Barbara's wine country consists of the towns of Santa Ynez, Los Olivos, Lompoc, Los Alamos, Buellton, and Santa Maria. These small farming communities are often overlooked in favor of the surrounding beach communities. But underneath their small-town charm is a big equestrian history, a rustic Western lifestyle, and even Prohibition-era ideals and temperance movements—ironic for the now thriving wine industry.

## Hello, My Name Is . . .

**Buellton** was founded by Rufus Thompson Buell, who owned the 27,000-acre Buell Ranch. By 1875 it already had a general store, post office, cheese factory, and worker housing. But Buellton didn't officially exist until 1920.

**Lompoc** has only a few things going for it. One is the wine ghetto, which is a positive thing, and the other is the penitentiary, which is . . . well, I guess a positive thing. One of the more remote areas of the county, its association with Vandenberg Air Force Base is partly what keeps it going.

**Los Olivos** is a wine taster's dream and a local's nightmare. More than forty-eight wine-tasting rooms compete for attention in a four-block radius. There are no stoplights here, and only a few stop signs, but summers are packed and the town is overrun with, well, people like you. If you don't like wine, why are you here? There are a few art galleries (the town used to be known for them) and a few very good restaurants.

**Santa Maria** is the workhorse of the agricultural area in Santa Barbara County. Driving through Santa Maria, you'll see fields and vineyards on both sides of Highway 101, and it's easy to assume it's merely a farming region. But Santa Maria also has a strong Western history, not to mention the now famous Santa Maria tri-tip barbeque. There is a reasonable wine community here, but it's spread out.

**Santa Ynez** has always been a laid-back horse and farming community, unaffected by time. That it is now the gateway to the wine region doesn't detract from its agrarian roots. It's small and cute, but then you need to move on to something else.

## The Mystery of History

**Lompoc** started as a Chumash village, and the name means something to the effect of "lagoon," or "still, stagnant waters." It was founded in 1874 as a temperance community (as in people who thought alcohol was evil), which is ironic in that the main tourist draw now is the Lompoc Wine Ghetto. Not to be confused with an actual ghetto, this is an urban winemaking spot, with more than seventeen tiny wineries operating behind roll-up doors in an old business park (without the customary ghetto graffiti). La Purisima Mission is here, and the city has about sixty outdoor murals and a bunch (pun intended) of flower farms.

**Los Alamos** means "poplars or cottonwoods," but the town also has a nickname, "little LA." The LA stands for Los Angeles; one of the reasons the town is now booming is that many LA folks showed up with wads of cash and bought second homes here. Before the Hollywood types arrived, the Chumash people had a village here until the early 1800s, when they left for the missions. The town, as we know it today, was founded in 1876. Today the train that once ran through it is no more, but electric vehicles now flock here for food, wine, beer, and more food.

**Los Olivos** got its start in 1861 with the establishment of the Overland/Coast Line Stage Station at Ballard. Actually, it was more a loose aggregate of residences. The true town didn't begin to form until 1887, when Felix Mattei, a Swiss-Italian immigrant, anticipated the arrival of the Pacific Coast Railway and opened a hotel to accommodate rail and stage passengers making connections in Los Olivos. The streets were graded by Chinese workers from the railroads. With the first whistle of the engine in November 1887, Los Olivos, while still small, was finally on the map. The 1882 Keenan/Hartley home is the oldest wooden home in Los Olivos and is a Santa Barbara County landmark.

**Santa Maria** was originally home to the Chumash people. In 1769, the Spanish Portola exploration party came through the Santa Maria Valley, signaling the advent of Mission San Luis Obispo in 1772 and Mission La Purisima in 1787. Settlers soon followed, looking for free land. By the time California achieved statehood in 1850, the Santa Maria Valley was one of the most productive agricultural areas in California, and farming is still a key component of the economy (try the strawberries and broccoli). Between 1869 and 1874, four of the valley's prominent settlers combined forty acres of land where their properties met to form a four-square-mile city, originally called Grangerville, centered on today's Main Street and Broadway. It was renamed Santa Maria (thankfully) in 1905. The Santa Maria Valley saw its share of oil exploration beginning in 1888, leading to large oil discoveries by the turn of the century. In 1901, William Orcutt urged his company, Union Oil, to lease more than seventy thousand acres. For the next eight decades, thousands of oil wells were drilled and put into production, facilitating growth for the city. By 1957 there were almost eighteen hundred oil wells in operation in the Santa Maria Valley, producing $60 million worth of oil. You can still see some of the old wells, but more likely you'll see vineyards and row crops, and chances are you'll eat and drink the bounty of Santa Maria wherever you dine.

**Santa Ynez** was called New Town—how creative was that?—when it was founded in 1882. Santa Ynez retains its historical Western flavor, with some of its storefronts still intact. By 1889, the town had become the focal point of the Santa Ynez Valley, both socially and economi- cally, complete with mercantile stores, blacksmith shops, garages, grocery stores, a barber shop, a harness shop, a millinery shop, and several saloons. The College Hotel was once the area's main lodging establishment, complete with a Victorian design and sixteen roof turrets. The hotel, which stood on Sagunto Street just south of Edison Street, hosted guests from all over the world. Not no more.

## Weird and Trivial . . . But True!

ⓘ Bill Cates, former owner of Tantara Winery, owned a horse named Tantara. When Tantara got on in years, he made the difficult decision to put her down and arranged for a vet to euthanize her. A month later, while Cates was visiting Tantara's grave, something bumped him from behind. It was Tantara—the vet had put down the wrong horse. Why the long face?

ⓘ In 1924, film director Cecil B. DeMille filmed the epic *The Ten Commandments*, constructing the largest set in movie history, called the City of the Pharaoh, in the dunes at Guadalupe. The set was 120 feet high and 720 feet long, employed 1,500 workers, and used half a million feet of lumber. Workers built three hundred chariots and had sev- enty-five miles of reinforcing cable to steady the massive structure. Additionally, 125 cooks turned out meals for three thousand actors, and we assume someone fed the five thousand animals. When filming was completed, the entire set was dismantled and *buried* in the dunes. And there it lay for the next six decades. By the mid-1980s, the hunt was on to find the remains of the set, then called the Lost City of DeMille. Ground-penetrating radar confirmed its existence. Explorers tried, mostly in vain, to bring the set to the surface, but because it was constructed of plaster of Paris sections simply fell apart. A few items have been recovered and are on display at the Guadalupe Dunes Center. The explorers recovered more cough syrup bottles than anything else. Why? This was during Prohibition, and cough syrup, at 13 percent alcohol, was certainly happy juice—especially way out in Guadalupe.

ⓘ Teeny tiny Ballard placed an 1887 advertisement in a San Francisco newspaper touting "choice lots for sale" ranging from seventy-five to three hundred bucks. These days, that's just a nice dinner.

ⓘ Goats don't fly, and neither do pigs. But Norm Yost, owner of Flying Goat Cellars, had pygmy goats on his property, and Norm built a nice little house for them. Some of the goats liked to climb on the roof of their domicile and jump off. Goats may be weird, but they inspired the perfect name for Yost's pinot noirs.

ⓘ Pea Soup Anderson's in Buellton was originally called Anderson Electrical Café because it was the first all-electric kitchen. Well, AC come, DC go.

ⓘ The Guadalupe-Nipomo Dunes area was poised in 1910 to become "the future Atlantic City of the Pacific," with a boardwalk and hotel. Investors were ecstatic. But that damn wind-blown sand kept shifting. By 1917, the few constructed buildings were abandoned. Enter the Dunites, a weird group of disenfranchised nomads and misfits who scavenged said buildings and built their own community. Edward St. Claire, a Spanish-American war veteran turned poet, was one of the first Dunites. Next was George Blais, a reformed alcoholic turned evangelist who dressed in a loincloth and bandana when he went into town. And there was flamboyant astrologer, writer, and socialite Gavin Arthur, grandson of US president Chester A. Arthur. The Dunites published their own magazine, with contributions from photographers such as Ansel Adams. The magazine, just like their bohemian lifestyle, eventually blew away, just like the sand they lived on.

ⓘ Neverland. Yes, the late pop star Michael Jackson built his famed theme park house here. No, you can't see it. All that is visible is a small guard shack and gate, and people leave mementos there. I think someone might have left Mentos—I'm not sure.

ⓘ In 1986 Los Olivos was renamed, for one day only, as Mayberry. The town was used for a photo shoot for the TV film return to Mayberry based on the beloved *Andy Griffith Show*.

ⓘ Santa Maria's first oil well, named Old Maude, was installed in 1904. During its first hundred days of operation, it sucked up a million barrels of oil. Now that's slick.

## Arts and Galleries

**Gallery Los Olivos** (gallerylosolivos.com, 2920 Grand Ave., 805/688-7517) This gallery acts as an artist's co-op, with the artists themselves running the show. They showcase about forty regional artists from within Santa Barbara County who work with wood, acrylic, ceramic, and pastels to create both traditional and abstract works of art. The artists rotate monthly solo shows. This is the largest gallery in what was once a thriving arts community. Stop and see what you might like in your home.

## Festivals and Events

**The Celebration of Harvest** (sbcountywines.com, November, $75 and up) This annual event celebrates the conclusion of the harvest in, roughly, October. The Chumash people had a harvest ceremony known as the Hutash that lasted for several days, but they didn't drink expensive wine and then climb into their Volvos and stay in fancy digs. This version is all about drinking—er, sipping—and, assuming you're paying attention, finding new wine and wineries you may not have heard of. This is a smaller version of the Vintner's Festival, with way smaller crowds and fewer tickets.

**Chumash Inter-Tribal Pow Wow** (santaynezchumash.org) This event allows the public to attend and watch traditional tribal dances and drumming circles and learn about Native American culture via speakers and literature. Native arts and crafts are for sale, and you'll have the chance to expand your knowledge of the Chumash and other tribal cultures. It's free to attend, but there is a small parking fee. It is typically held in late September.

**Santa Maria Valley Strawberry Festival** (santamariafairpark. com, 937 S. Thornburg St., 805/925-8824) This festival is held over three days in April. There are more strawberries than you've ever seen—no, I'm serious. Strawberries are one of the top three crops in Santa Maria, and what better way to celebrate that fun fact than by eating them? There are food booths, live bands, and the chance to sample different strawberry varieties (betcha didn't know there are more than six hundred varieties), including strawberry desserts. It's berry fun.

**Vintner's Festival** (sbcountywines.com) Held the third weekend in April, this is the granddaddy of the wine events, with nearly three thousand people showing up. More than three dozen wineries, a dozen food booths, local arts and crafts, live local bands, a silent auction—it's non-stop food and wine, at least for a few hours. Many wineries and tasting rooms offer special incentives, and this five-day event just keeps getting bigger. It's a big, loud party. If you like that sort of energy, this is a great way to celebrate and discover new wines.

## Health and Wellness

**The Spa at Chumash Casino Resort** (chumashcasino.com, 3400 Highway 246, Santa Ynez, 805/686-0855) This is the most comprehensive spa in the Santa Maria Valley, and there is nothing like it between Santa Barbara and San Luis Obispo. This is the only five-diamond service you'll find. The spa commands 4,500 square feet of space, with multiple treatment rooms, massive men's and women's locker rooms, an outdoor pool and hot tub, and an indoor fitness room. The spa offers seven types of massage. The full-body massage (either fifty or eighty minutes) is the most popular offering here. It combines the long, slow strokes of Swedish massage with the pinpoint accuracy of deep-tissue massage to get those kinks out. You'll also find everything from maternity/pregnancy massage to the stone massage, which features heated local river stones used in conjunction with sage massage oil to cleanse and relax. (Native Americans have traditionally burned sage, but that's a specific odor: hint—pot is now legal in California.) As an alternative, a foot massage using reflexology will hit the pressure points on your feet.

## Museums

**Guadalupe-Nipomo Dunes Center** (dunescenter.org, 1065 Guadalupe St., Guadalupe, 805/343-2455) The center is

*This set was buried in the dunes. Artifacts on display at Dunes Center.*

housed in a converted 1910 Craftsman house with beautiful wood built-ins, which hold the research library. Staff here know best how to explore the eighteen miles of coastline and the 22,000 acres that encompass the dunes complex. If you're a birder or off-roader, or if you just want to walk the beach, contact them to find the spots best suited to your needs. Small exhibit spaces highlight whale bones, a brief history of the area and dunes, and—most visited of all—the history of the set of the 1956 film *The Ten Commandments*, which was filmed at the dunes (see Weird and Trivial . . . But True!).

**Santa Maria Valley Historical Society Museum** (616 S. Broadway, Santa Maria, 805/922-3130, free) This impressive little museum is mainly focused on Santa Maria's heritage. You'll find a variety of old-time things, such as a 1930s phone switchboard; an actual hanging noose with dried blood still visible; info on the city's most famous food, tri-tip; and odds and ends from the area. But there's also a complete skeleton of a saber-toothed tiger, which perished in the famous La Brea Tar Pits in LA. (We don't have tar pits in Santa Barbara. We had Brad Pitt, but that's another sinking feeling.) The museum also has a collection of Civil War and post-Civil War letters, including a few items from Mary Todd Lincoln, George Armstrong Custer, and Abraham Lincoln's son, Robert Lincoln.

**Santa Ynez Valley Historical Museum** and **Parks-Janeway Carriage House** (santaynezmuseum.org, 3596 Sagunto St., Santa Ynez, 805/688-7889, $5) These two museums do an admirable job of presenting local history. There's a good-sized diorama with a narrow-gauge train that creeps its way around the track, showing how the train depot near Mattie's Tavern used to look back in the day. Okay, it's not high tech, but it is kind of fun. There are also small displays in the Valley Room showing the original five small towns of Solvang (1911), Santa Ynez (1882), Los Olivos (1887), Ballard (1881), and Buellton (1920). These are short histories but are part of the development of the Valley. The pioneer room showcases well-appointed interior furnishings of the day. The carriage house is an impressive collection of all types of carriages, surreys, and wagons, including an old fire wagon and a popcorn wagon from 1909, which sold nuts and fresh-popped popcorn. These carriages are in fantastic shape; obviously they have been well cared for. You'll also find a selection of tack and saddles—if you don't know what these are, don't worry about it. The Pioneer Room is outfitted with turn-of-the-century furnishings, many from local ranches.

## Nightlife

**Costa de Oro Friday Night Wine Downs** (cdowinery.com, 1331 S. Nicholson Ave., Santa Maria, 805/922-1468) Every Friday evening from 5 p.m. to 8 p.m., local musicians pour into the wine-tasting room (that was pretty bad). It's a festive, fun gathering, and live music goes with your wine by the glass, by the bottle, or on tap. You might see a singer-songwriter or three guys jamming classic rock; there's a rotating assortment of music here. There's no cover charge, but the various foods, such as fried chicken or sliders for around $15, sell quickly. It's a good idea to RSVP for the food so it's there for you.

## Outdoor Activities

**Cachuma Lake Recreation Area** (countyofsb.org/parks/cachuma.sbc, 2225 Highway 154, 805/606-5055) Built in 1953 to provide a reservoir for Santa Barbara's water needs, the lake covers three thousand acres and has forty-two miles of shoreline. Because this is a source of drinking water for people like me, there is no swimming allowed, nor any body contact with the water, thank you very much. There is a fully stocked general store, which has firewood, canned foods, clothing, and even a small selection of magazines and books. There's also a gas station, coin laundry, hot showers, fishing piers, and plenty of hiking and biking trails. For those who prefer to camp, there are several options. Single-family campsites are first come, first served. More than four hundred campsites, one hundred with full electrical, water, and sewer hookups and thirty with electrical and water hookups, can accommodate any size RV. Each campsite contains a picnic table and fire ring, with showers, restrooms, and potable water nearby. An RV dump station is also available. The campsites book out early, so if you're considering this option you need to plan ahead.

## AIR

**Santa Barbara Soaring** (sbsoaring.com, 900 Airport Rd., Santa Ynez, 805/688-2517) This outfit offers glider rides over wine country (but you're not consuming wine as you do this). It's an amazing experience to float above the region and not only see the vineyards but also get a better understanding of the topography of the land. Santa Barbara

Soaring has been operating for more than twenty years and takes any age, from 4 to 104. Flights last fifteen to thirty minutes. A plane tows the glider up, along with you and a pilot—that's all—and then drops the tow-line so you're soaring above the earth without the noise of engines, making this a relatively quiet and very scenic experience. Of course, everything ultimately depends on the weather, and whether you can handle small spaces.

## EARTH

**Nojoqui Falls Park** (countyofsb.org/parks/day-use/nojoqui-falls.sbc, 3250 Alisal Rd., Goleta, 805/568-2460) We have very few waterfalls in Santa Barbara County. I mean, we have the entire Pacific Ocean at our disposal, but waterfalls here are typically at the end of a long hike. Oh well, can't have everything. But a two-mile drive off Highway 101 will bring you to this park, which is spacious enough to accommodate RVs, fire pits, barbecues, picnic tables, and large grassy areas. A ten-minute walk will get you to the falls with a small elevation gain. Because the falls are seasonal, there may or may not be water; if there is, it's typically just enough to get your feet wet. But even without water it's a beautiful, leisurely hike.

**Rancho Oso Horseback Riding** (thousandtrails.com/california/rancho-oso-rv-camping-resort/, 3750 Paradise Rd., 877/570-2267) This three-hundred acres of wilderness offers a variety of horseback-riding options. The one-hour trail ride starts at $40, and though your horse isn't roaming free it's still a nice, if predictable, ride through the back country. You will cross streams and see a few Chumash artifacts (as this was a Chumash village site long ago) as you meander the lower canyons. Longer rides offer scenic vistas, but the lumbering pace of the horses can get annoying after a while.

**La Purisima Golf Course** (lapurisimagolf.com, 3455 E. Highway 246, Lompoc, 805/735-8395) This eighteen-hole, par-seventy-two course was designed by Robert Graves, who also designed Sandpiper in Santa Barbara and Hunter Ranch in Paso Robles. It's moderately priced and has a small grill and pro shop. This is a tough course, with more hills than most any other course and brisk, cool winds in the afternoon; in other words, challenging is an understatement. But if you're up for it, in spite of its rather remote location, it will be worth your effort. Like many courses on the Central Coast, it has an abundance of oak trees to contend with.

**Vino Vaqueros** (vinovaqueros.com, 2178 Mora Ave., Santa Ynez, 805/944-0493) Imagine you and your horse out for a ride, tasting wine. Imagine your horse doesn't drink, which is a good thing, because you're riding across vineyards and chaparral-covered hillsides with other people who like wine. Vino Vaqueros will take you to some exclusive properties, and it offers rides sans wine if you and your horse are teetotalers.

## FIRE

We discourage fires anywhere in the Valley because we have a treacherous fire season—and that's no joke. The Cachuma Lake Recreation Area has fire rings, so you can enjoy those, but otherwise fires are only allowed in designated places.

## WATER

### Cachuma Lake Nature Cruises

Cruises are conducted by park employees and are a great way to see the lake and surrounding area without any effort. The two-hour cruises get you onboard a covered thirty-passenger pontoon boat called the Osprey. A naturalist (fully clothed) is on board to speak about the environment and wildlife and answer questions. The wildlife cruise runs March to October and focuses on animals such as deer and bears, as well as the plants that make the lake their home. It's a wonderful outing to get an up-close look at the shoreline and learn about the wildlife and history of the habitat, but make sure you bring a wrap, as it can get cool in certain parts of the lake. The eagle cruise runs November to February, and the focus is on bald eagles and osprey, both of which live here. There's also a greater concentration during these months on migratory birds.

### Cachuma Lake Fishing

Because of the lake bottom's topography, shallow areas, and aquatic plant beds, this is a great habitat for fish. During non-drought years (yeah, right), the lake supports populations of large-mouth and small-mouth bass, and I don't mean the chatty kind. There's also the ill-named crappie and bluegill, red-ear sunfish, channel catfish, and rainbow trout. You can rent gear at the bait shop in the marina.

### Cachuma Lake Boating

You can bring your own boat to the launch ramp located at the marina or rent a boat on an hourly, half-day, daily, weekly, monthly, or annual basis. The recreation area has outboards, rowboats, pontoons, and paddle boats. Day rental rates range from $30 per hour for a four-passenger rowboat all the way up to $385 per day for a pontoon accommodating twenty passengers. You can launch your own vessel from the four launch ramps or small harbor at the marina. Early spring mornings are great: Bring hot cocoa, get in the water before the sun rises, and wait for the warmth of a new day to liberate you.

## Sites: Historic

### Misión La Purisima Concepcion de Maria Santisima

(lapurisimamission.org, 2295 Purisima Rd., Lompoc, 805/733-3713, $6) The long Spanish name of this place translates to the Mission of the Immaculate Conception of Most Holy Mary (say that three times fast). It was founded

December 8, 1787, and constructed in the traditional quadrangle mission shape, with the converted Chumash living outside the mission walls. On the morning of December 21, 1812, an earthquake destroyed the mission, and the exposed adobe walls dissolved in the winter rains (please sing "Dust in the Wind" by Kansas at this point). Those plucky padres rebuilt (actually the Indians rebuilt) the mission, but they abandoned the traditional design in favor of a linear design. All was fine and well until violence erupted in 1824 at La Purisima with a Chumash revolt. Soldiers guarding the missions throughout the Central Coast were poorly paid because Spain didn't pay its bills—kind of like now. Soldiers took their frustrations out on the Native American population, specifically by beating a Chumash person from La Purisima who was stationed at Mission Santa Ines. That didn't sit well with the Chumash, and Native Americans from all three Santa Barbara missions got ticked off and rose up in armed revolt. Spanish soldiers from Monterey overtook La Purisima by force, leaving sixteen Native Americans dead and several wounded. The terms of surrender were eventually negotiated, but seven Native Americans who surrendered were

*Mission La Purisima*

executed; twelve others were sentenced to hard labor at the Santa Barbara presidio.

Secularization killed off the mission system, and church services ceased here in 1836. Buildings fell into disrepair, and in 1845 the mission was sold for just over a thousand dollars. Eventually it was used as a stable. La Purisima was rescued in 1934 and is now part of the California State Parks system. Some people believe it's haunted; others think it just makes for good TV. Regardless, it's one of the coolest missions on the Central Coast precisely because it's so different from the others. Sitting on two thousand acres, it has hiking trails and a five-acre garden, which displays native and domestic plants typical of a mission garden, including fig and olive trees and a wide variety of plants, such as sage and Spanish dagger. There are also mission animals typical of the times, such as burros, horses, long-horn cattle, sheep, goats, and turkeys (not the original ones, of course), which are displayed in a corral in the main compound. The mission is actually three buildings with well over a dozen rooms, including soldiers' sleeping quarters, the weaving shop, the candle-making room, the chapel, and the priests' quarters. Many of the rooms still have their original dirt floors; this is the best mission to visit for an authentic experience.

## Sites: Not Exactly Historic

**Figueroa Mountain** This mountain tops out at 4,528 feet, and the views from here are pretty killer. As Figueroa Mountain Drive peels off from Route 154 near Los Olivos, it takes you away from cute little towns and deposits you in the middle of chaparral-covered hills and lots of oak trees. Yes, this is where Michael Jackson's Neverland Ranch is located, but trust me, you can't see anything, just a non-descript gate on the left-hand side of the road, about six miles from the turnoff of Highway 154. Making your way toward the foothills, the first things that begin to disappear

178

are the oak trees. Here you'll find pine trees, wildflowers, and more pronounced rock formations. From the lookout tower on top of the mountain, you've got cool 360-degree views of much of the county. The Santa Ynez Mountains are to the south, and from this perspective they appear as a solid mountain wall. On a clear day, typically from February to April, the Channel Islands shimmer on the horizon. The foreground is the Santa Ynez Valley. Above and to the west is Point Conception, a land revered by the Chumash, the place of the setting sun, where these Native Americans believed they would travel in the life that comes after death—though frankly I'd choose Europe. You can descend the way you came, or if you're adventurous, and depending on the type of car you have, you can continue along some bumpy roads and over streams and eventually merge with Happy Canyon Road, making this a thirty-mile loop. This is not a short drive, but it offers some spectacular scenery.

**Vandenberg Air Force Base** (vandenberg.af.mil, Highway 1 at Black Rd., 805/606-3595) The base offers tours that include the Heritage Museum, which has mock-ups of missile silos, an old missile control station, and decommissioned rocket engines, as well as a visit to Space Launch Complex 10 (isn't that a 1980s band?). Tours last about three hours: drive times around this massive military installation of 99,000 acres consume a lot of that. Public tours are offered by the Public Affairs Office, and reservations are required several weeks in advance. Information on Vandenberg rocket launches—yes, people get up to watch rockets go off—is available on the base's website. Launch days and times are released several days in advance and tend to be in the early morning hours because of weather and visibility.

The US Army took over the land in 1941, and it was a training camp for our boys during World War II. Perhaps weirdly, German and Italian prisoners of war were sent here. To help alleviate the severe labor shortage in the commercial market created by the war, some of the German prisoners worked in local communities, mainly in agricultural jobs, such as picking grapes. A maximum-security disciplinary barrack was constructed on the property in 1946, specifically for military prisoners—now it's the United States Penitentiary at Lompoc.

In 1957 the base was re-purposed as the nation's first space and ballistic missile training base. Vandenberg is the only military base in the US from which unmanned government and commercial satellites are launched into orbit. It's also the only site from which intercontinental ballistic missiles are test fired into the Pacific Ocean (with apologies to anyone vacationing in Hawaii). The missiles land (hopefully) at the Kwajalein Atoll near the Marshall Islands. Besides its size, remoteness from heavily populated areas, and moderate climate that affords year-round operations, Vandenberg's coastal location allows these missiles to be launched without any negative impact over populated areas . . . at least, this is what they tell us.

## Eat AND Drink

### Bars

**The Tap Room** (santamariainn.com, 801 S. Broadway, Santa Maria, 805/928-7777) Located inside the Santa Maria Inn built in 1941, this is a very cool old spot, with leather chairs, semi-private booths, and an old-fashioned bar and fireplace somewhat reminiscent of an English pub. There's live music most weekends; weeknights tend to be quiet, you know, so you can actually talk. The drinks are standard, but the ambience is wonderful.

### Restaurants and Food

**Bell Street Farm** $$, L-D (bellstreetfarm.com, 406 Bell St., Los Alamos, 805/344-4609) Run by a couple of LA guys and housed in the 1916 Bank of Italy (the restaurant, not the guys), the interior is quaint and casual, with a bright pressed-tin ceiling reflecting a country store atmosphere. There's an outdoor back patio with rustic picnic tables—charming and very country. This place serves a lot of sandwiches and soups made with organic ingredients, although they're a little on the pricey side (it's an old bank, after all). But frankly there's not much else around here, as Los Alamos is an outpost between Solvang and Santa Maria. I love the tamarind chicken, meatloaf sandwich, and peanut-butter icebox pie.

**Bob's Well Bread Bakery** $$, B-L (bobswellbread.com, 550 Bell St., Los Alamos, 805/344-3000) Bob makes, well, bread. Bob, a former Sony Television Pictures exec, got laid off from his bread-and-butter job, and he needed dough so he started making bread. If you want something resembling a French bakery in Northern Santa Barbara County, this is it. This is all fresh-baked bread and pastries and buttery, flaky croissants. There's a full menu for a sit down, as well as grab-and-go food, such as a demi baguette with ham and cheese and house-made butter. Or grab a loaf of artisan bread. This spot, formerly cabins, then a restaurant, and then a biker bar, has history. The floors are original Douglas fir, and this feels like an original, intimate bakery. There's plenty of outdoor seating.

**Far Western Tavern** $$ B-L-D (farwesterntavern.com, 300 E. Clark Ave., Orcutt, 805/937-2211) The Far Western is known for grilling most of its foods over red oak. Dinners begin with warm and spicy jalapeño cheddar rolls. Start your food odyssey with the oak-grilled short rib taco, a sturdy, crisp shell filled with rich, earthy meat and mildly spicy poblano peppers, sitting on cheese grits. The oak-grilled scallop is a medium scallop wrapped in bacon with a maple-Dijon cream sauce. The oak-grilled romaine salad is a quarter head of romaine topped with bacon blue-cheese vinaigrette.

**Hitching Post** $$$, D (hitchingpost1.com, 3325 Point Sal Rd., Casmalia, 805/937-6151) Located in the middle of nowhere, the Hitching Post opened as a restaurant in 1944, after serving as a hotel for more than two decades. Now, I should tell you it's unimpressive inside—and outside, frankly—but it's cool because nothing stands out . . . except the food. It's small, dark, and moody without trying to be. Animal heads and all manner of saws hang on the walls, but you don't come here for the architectural elements. You can see the grill and otherwise absorb the restaurant's quaint nature. Get the top sirloin; all dinners come with a crudité plate, shrimp cocktail, salad with house-made dressing, and garlic bread. It's plenty of food. Its sister restaurant, **Hitching Post II** (hitchingpost2.com, 406 E. Highway 246, Buellton, 805/688-0676), is the one everyone knows; it was used in the film *Sideways* and is located right off Highway 101 in Buellton. For all intents and purposes, it's identical to the original, but it's a little more upscale. Both get crowded, and for good reason.

**Sides Hardware and Shoes** $$, L-D (brothersrestaurant.com, 2375 Alamo Pintado Ave., Los Olivos, 805/688-4820) This building was built in 1901 as a hardware and shoe store, owned by Mr. Sides. Sounds like a pitch for a sitcom. Burgers, salads, and sandwiches are on offer, and if any dish comes with the restaurant's bacon steak, order it! It's thick but tender, cured with maple syrup, brown sugar, and salt and then slow cooked. If you're a bacon lover (if you're not, put this book down immediately!), you'll be a happy porker here. The fried Brussels sprouts are also pretty amazing.

**Sissy's Uptown Café** $$, L-D (sissysuptowncafe.com, 112 S. I St., Lompoc, 805/735-4877) A stalwart in Lompoc, this place never disappoints. Standards like the Nicoise salad and French-dip sandwich are consistent, and all the desserts are house-made daily. The café also has a huge selection of local wines, quite an impressive list for a place this small and out of the way. If you're in Lompoc, do seek it out.

**Vineyard House** $$, B-L-D (thevineyardhouse.com, 3631 Sagunto St., Santa Ynez, 805/688-2886) This is a converted 1907 residence. Creative, flavorful food comes out of this kitchen on a regular basis, including the baked brie, which is always a treat, as is the crispy buttermilk chicken and a hearty, thick venison verde chili. The restaurant makes its own soups and salad dressings, as well as desserts like the eternally decadent and gooey molten chocolate cake. The interior is homey and intimate, but the prime seating on nice days is the outside deck, where the pepper trees hang languidly over the tables.

## *Italian*

**S.Y. Kitchen** $$, L-D (sykitchen.com, 1110 Faraday St., Santa Ynez, 805/691-9794) This restaurant has a rustic interior and covered side patio. You'll hear the strains of Italian being spoken inside. There is indoor seating facing the bar, two side rooms, and a few outdoor tables. Though it lacks much decorative definition, the restaurant does feel intimate and homey. Dinners begin with thick, lightly grilled sourdough bread and olive oil, and crudités composed of celery, red peppers, cucumbers, and carrots. From there, a wealth of fresh pasta dishes are bursting with flavor. Make sure you get the tiramisu for dessert; it's presented in a mason jar.

## *Mexican*

**Dos Carlitos Restaurant & Tequila Bar** $$, L-D (doscarlitosrestaurant.com, 3544 Sagunto St., Santa Ynez, 805/688-0033) This restaurant boasts high, vaulted ceilings and a nice outdoor patio. The furnishings were made in Mexico, and the place has an authentic feel. It serves Mexican food, such as hand-made tortillas, with a steep price tag. Sit at the copper-topped bar and try one of sixty tequilas by the shot, ranging in price from $9 to $36. Awesome, diverse salsas and the rock shrimp tacos are killer. It can get loud inside, but the food is terrific. On summer nights grab a seat outdoors.

**El Sitio** $, L-D (35 W. Highway 246, Buellton, 805/688-3707) Sometimes you don't want fancy wine country food; you just want something inexpensive, hearty, quick, and easy. Well, ta-da! El Sitio is a small taqueria serving immensely flavorful tacos and small meals. Located right off Highway 101, it's easy to miss because it's so tiny. The corn tortillas are rolled out and grilled when you order, and the simple fillings of cheese, chorizo, pork, chicken, fish, and even beef tongue and the like are then adorned by you at a small salsa bar. A few bucks, tasty food, and you're on your way!

### Sandwiches

**Panino** $, L (paninorestaurants.com, 2900 Grand Ave., Los Olivos, 805/688-9304) A small local chain throughout Santa Barbara County, Panino's does terrific sandwiches and salads; this outpost best serves wine country. Sometimes you don't want a full sit-down meal; you simply want a quick bite to eat, or maybe something to take on the road. Well, here it is. The sandwiches and salads are made to order, and there is a good selection of vegetarian options. The roast turkey and brie sandwich is a personal favorite, as is the avocado and provolone with fresh basil and honey mustard. This chain has multiple locations, including in Montecito, downtown Santa Barbara, and Goleta.

### Sweets

**Gina's Piece of Cake** (ginaspieceofcake.com, 307 Town Center East, Santa Maria, 805/922-7866) Don't you love a bakery where you can smell the sweet cake icing a mile away? If you don't, skip to the next section. Otherwise, if you're in Santa Maria, Gina's does beautiful custom cakes and bakes brownies, cookies, muffins, éclairs, bagels, and breads. The bakery is located just inside the Santa

Maria Mall, and yes, we all need a piece of cake once in a while—so come here for your bakery fix.

## Wines, Brews, and Spirits

The first documented viticulture in California dates from 1779 at Mission San Gabriel in Southern California, and eventually grapes were grown throughout the mission system. The so-called "mission grape," a hybrid of different types, was high in sugar content and low in acid and produced a thin, sweet wine that by many accounts wasn't good—maybe something like Two Buck Chuck. But the mission grape dominated the industry until the end of California's Mexican era in the late 1840s, in part because there wasn't anything else. Wine and brandy production was a significant source of income for some of the missions. Old Mission Santa Barbara established a vineyard and winery in the 1830s. Grapes were used to make not only wine but also raisins, which were handy food for travelers, kind of like early trail mix. But grape production wasn't limited to the missions. Around 1820, San Antonio Winery was built in what is now Goleta. The lonely historic adobe winery is still standing nearly two hundred years later, though it's on private property, which I have visited. Another commercial winery, the Packard Winery, was built in 1865, also in Santa Barbara, and in the late 1890s about two hundred acres of grapes were being turned into wine on Santa Cruz Island (there are rumors that some winemakers are still pulling grapes off the island). Near Mission La Purisima in Lompoc grapes were planted in the 1880s, and a few of those vines survive today, though they are now on private property. The first post-Prohibition commercial grapevine plantings were done in the 1960s and 1970s in the Santa Maria Valley. Currently, sixty-four varieties of grapes are planted throughout the county on 21,000 acres. Pinot noir and chardonnay are the most widely planted varieties. The wine industry in Santa Barbara County is thriving, in spite of the fluctuations of the economy, transitional markets, fickle consumers, and inconsistent harvests.

## A Note on Wine Tasting in the Valley

The Valley is a large area, and clusters of wine-tasting rooms are spread out. It's best to stick with one area rather than attempting the long drives between them. Solvang has its own (walkable) tasting rooms, as do Los Olivos (forty-eight of them, and it's a mess in the summer) and Lompoc. For pinot and chardonnay, the Santa Rita Hills are ground zero. For Rhone, Ballard Canyon; for Bordeaux, Happy Canyon. Everything else is all over the map, so a little planning will yield a productive day.

**Ascendant Spirits** (ascendantspirits.com, 37 Industrial Way, Buellton, 805/691-1000) Ascendant was founded by owner Stephen Gertman. This former producer of automotive shows for ESPN, Speed, and the History Channel wanted a change, so he made a left turn, career-wise. The tasting room is located in Buellton on a dead-end street, and you'll find his Breaker Bourbon, Silver Lightning Moonshine, and Caviar Lime Vodka. Get up to speed and check out Santa Barbara's first post-Prohibition distillery. Tours and tastings run Friday through Sunday.

**Bridlewood** (bridlewoodestatewinery.com, 3555 Roblar Ave., Santa Ynez, 805/688-9000) This is one of the most picturesque vineyards around. Bridlewood used to be a thoroughbred horse farm, hence the winery name and horse logo. A long driveway unveils a Mission-style bell tower standing like a sentinel above lush grounds, reminding you that this was once a grand estate. There are still horses on the expansive grounds, and an original racetrack is still located behind the winery near a large pond.

Bridlewood's tasting room reflects the wood and earthen tones of an equestrian facility, complete with high ceilings. The Central Coast is an extraordinary place that is home to some of the best grapes California has to offer; because Bridlewood collaborates with vintners from Monterey, San Luis Obispo, and Santa Barbara County it is able to create handcrafted wine using a broad palette. And this is exactly what you'll find at the tasting room: unique blends; sturdy syrahs and rhone-style blends; Happy Canyon cabernet sauvignon; and estate-grown zinfandel, chardonnay, viognier, and pinot noir. Quit horsing around and check it out.

**Dierberg/Star Lane Winery** (starlanevineyard.com, 1280 Drum Canyon Rd., Lompoc, 805/697-1466) Its big ol' tasting room, a big ol' barn, is picture perfect, all by its lonesome. The Dierbergs operate three wine labels: Star Lane; their estate wines, called Dierberg; and the everyday-ish Three Saints label. All of these wines, at various price points, are excellent. The Star Lane sauvignon blanc is terrific, and the value-priced Three Saints wines, including merlot, cabernet sauvignon, and pinot noir, are best bets. The Dierbergs also own the Hermannhof Winery in Missouri, but that's another book.

**Dragonette Cellars** (dragonettecellars.com, 2445 Alamo Pintado Ave., Los Olivos, 805/693-0077) This may sound like a fancy, made-up stage name for a magician, but don't tell that to the Dragonette brothers. They, along with Brandon Sparks-Gillis create sauvignon blanc, various pinot noirs, and syrah and Rhone blends are outstanding. The staff is great; the little tasting room is on the sterile side, all wood toned and aloof, but once you sip the wines you won't notice anything else. If you stop in Los Olivos for a tasting, make certain you come here.

**Firestone Walker Brewery** (firestonewalker.com, 620 McMurray Rd., Buellton, 805/697-4777) While in wine country, you might need beer. Firestone Walker's beers really are the beer of the Central Coast. It brews in Paso Robles, but this outpost offers four alternating beers on tap. It also offers food, such as pork chops, steaks and burgers, and beer-battered fish and chips, which is a little on the pricey side. The casual, brewpub look of the former tasting room has been sanitized to look glitzy. No matter, Firestone Walker is the best brewery on the Central Coast. It is right off Highway 101, just north of Buellton. Grab a brew, and if your picky friend wants wine, the brewery pours Firestone wines by the glass.

**Flying Goat** (flyinggoatcellars.com, 1520 E. Chestnut Ct., Unit A, Lompoc, 805/736-9032) In addition to several iterations of beautifully seductive pinot noir, Flying Goat is locally known for Goat Bubbles, a light, delicate sparkling pinot noir. Owner Norm Yost goes for an uncommon restrained style with his wines, allowing the lush cherry and raspberry elements of his pinot noir grapes to express themselves and not be overwhelmed with too much oak. These are consistently excellent wines that avoid the bombastic, over-ripe characteristics that many area pinots exhibit. The tasting room is nothing to write home about, but his wines are.

**Foley Estates** (foleywines.com, 6121 E. Highway 246, Lompoc, 805/737-6222) You want superb pinot noir and chardonnay? You want a classy environment surrounded by acres of low rolling hills covered with vines? Here you go. You simply cannot go wrong here. These wines truly reflect their origin, the Santa Rita Hills, which is where you are when you're standing at Foley. It offers a private wine-and-cheese pairing in addition to a regular tasting. There are front and back patios for a picnic. The drawback is that the wines are quite pricey, but they are damn good.

**Larner** (larnerwine.com, 2900 Grand Ave., Los Olivos, 805/688-8148) Michael Larner is a geologist who loves dirt, yet his wines aren't dirty. He understood early on that Ballard Canyon would be ideal for syrah, grenache, and mourvèdre. His tiny tasting room has big wines, balanced beauties that truly reflect the small Ballard Canyon AVA. He's got twenty-three acres of syrah, in eleven sub-blocks, using seven clones, planted on three different rootstocks to play with (sounds like a math problem). Therefore, his syrahs straddle cool-climate pepper spice and warm-climate berry fruit, and they are some of the best coming out of Santa Barbara.

**Nagy Wines** (nagywines.com, 145 S. Gray St., Orcutt, 805/286-7228) Clarissa Nagy started her career as a food scientist and ended up in wine, which is still a food of sorts. Though her day job is as winemaker for Riverbench, she moonlights with her own small brand. You'll find viognier, pinot noir, and syrah in her small tasting room, which holds a few tables and stools. Her wines are lithe, unobtrusive, and quietly seductive. The tasting room has gifty items, as well.

**Palmina** (palminawines.com, 1520 E. Chestnut Ct., Lompoc, 805/735-2030) I hate the term Cal-Ital, a reference to Italian grapes grown in California. Sure, we grow them here, but they're unlike their Italian cousins because of way too many factors to go into here. On the plus side, Palmina makes the best Italian varieties on the entire Central Coast: delicate Dolcetto, burly Barbera, tasty Tocai Friulano, a rustic Rosato, and many more cool varieties. You'll find hands-down terrific wines that are something out of the norm for the area.

**Presqu'ile** (presquilewine.com, 5391 Presquile Dr., Santa Maria, 805/937-8110) Napa has its share of behemoth estates, but in Santa Barbara we don't do that. The closest we come is Presqu'ile, which is less behemoth and more massive, but scaled to its surroundings. It is undeniably popular because it is so well designed—expansive without being pretentious. Its wines—including pinot noir, chardonnay, sparkling wines, and syrah—are terrific, and it offers a number of events, concerts, and functions, in part because it can handle the crowds. A visit is worth the time.

**Riverbench** (riverbench.com, 6020 Foxen Canyon Rd., Santa Maria, 805/937-8340) Riverbench is all pinot noir, all the time. Okay, that's not exactly right; there's also chardonnay, a few sparklers the staff rarely talk about, and a riesling they never talk about. Aside from the beautiful property (a great picnic area when it's not overly windy, which is much of the time) and a cool tasting room (a Pottery Barn look), the pinot noirs here, while not inexpensive, are pure expressions of what pinot is supposed to be. Sure, you can find brutish, hefty examples elsewhere, but that is not pinot noir. The elegance, finesse, and subtle nature of the grape are treated properly here. That's not to say it's stuffy, but this is Santa Barbara County pinot, and she's treated lady-like.

**Sanford** (sanfordwinery.com, 5010 Santa Rosa Rd., Lompoc, 800/426-9463) The first time Steve Fennell, winemaker for Sanford Winery, was on Santa Rosa Road, he was in a bike race. Little did he know that twenty-five years later he would be making wine on Santa Rosa Road. Sanford is one of Santa Barbara's oldest wineries and has always focused on pinot noir and chardonnay grown in the cooler Santa Rita Hills. Its wines are truly expressive of this climate and are definitely worth seeking out. There is a tasting room in downtown Santa Barbara, but the winery location is postcard wine country.

**Tercero** (tercerowines.com, 2445 Alamo Pintado Ave., Los Olivos, 805/245-9584) Larry Schaffer is a fan of Rhone wines, and his small tasting room is filled with unique wines and diverse interpretations of these wines. His syrahs are pretty spectacular, and his cabernet franc is like sticking your nose in a fresh berry pie. The small space is unremarkable visually, but that matters not. Larry is often in the tasting room, and he rotates his wines often so there are always new goodies to try. He also has a habit of baking bread, so you might find some cool, different breads to try while you're there.

## Antiques and Old Stuff

**Depot Antique Mall** (515 Bell St., Los Alamos, 805/344-3315) Once the depot for the Pacific Coast Railway, this huge place now holds more than sixty antique vendors in three large rooms. With everything from vintage posters to an abundance of furniture and collectables, it has reasonable prices and is worth the short drive. It's past Los Alamos, right off Highway 101 between Solvang and Santa Maria. Some items are knockoffs, but you'll find a wide selection of rotating items, especially the larger furniture pieces, so new stuff keeps showing up.

## Books and the Printed Realm

**Bookworm** (230 E. Betteravia Rd., Santa Maria, 805/922-4282) This is a great little bookstore, with used books stacked to the rafters at reasonable prices. The staff know their inventory like the backs of their hands, which is good because the place is so packed with books you may not be able to find the back of your hand. If you like the feeling of getting lost, here ya go.

## Clothes and Accessories

**New Image Thrift Store** (newimagethrift.com, 2512 S. Broadway, Santa Maria, 805/922-9668) The inventory is constantly changing here, and there are tons of clothes, CDs, coffee makers, knick-knacks, and whatnot. The place is clean and organized, but it's big, which means if you're a thrift store junkie, you'll be here for a few hours. They have a friendly staff, and you'll probably walk out with something.

## Specialty

**Clairmont Farms** (clairmontfarms.com, 2480 Roblar Ave., Los Olivos, 805/688-7505) This family-owned organic lavender farm is also home to 180-year-old olive trees originally planted by the Catholic padres—part of the grove that gave Los Olivos its name. You can observe the process of distilling lavender and learn all the ways this herb is used, be it essential oils or cooking herbs. The farm sells oils, teas, honey (yum), soaps, and more, all infused with lavender. There's even lavender shampoo for your dog, cat, or horse—after all, our pets should smell nice, right? (Good luck getting your horse in a shower for a shampoo.)

## I'm on a Budget

**Santa Maria Inn** (santamariainn.com, 801 S. Broadway, 805/928-7777) Constructed in 1917, this pet-friendly hotel has 164 rooms and 18 suites. You can stay in the historic part of the hotel or one of the newer rooms. Either way, the inn channels the turn of the century with the décor, Victorian furnishings, and lots of antiques. Located centrally in Santa Maria, it features a pretty good in-house restaurant and old tavern on its five acres of grounds. Santa Maria is ripe with chain hotels, so a visit here is hands down the better local experience. Besides, Clark Gable, Marilyn Monroe, Shirley Temple, and Jimmy Stewart have all stayed here. Now you can add your name to the ledger.

## Life Is Pretty Good

**Chumash Casino Resort** (chumashcasino.com, 3400 E. Highway 246, Santa Ynez, 800/248-6274) This resort is everything under one roof, including a 122-room hotel, day spa, gift shop, and small business center. And of course there's the casino itself, which consists of two thousand slots, a variety of poker tables (including a twenty-four-hour room), bingo games large enough for a thousand players, and blackjack. You do need to know that smoking is permitted inside the casino, but not in the hotel. There are three restaurants within the casino, and a 1,400-seat entertainment showroom brings in a solid lineup of performers and occasional boxing matches. The fitness room (one of the few in the entire Santa Ynez Valley) looks out to the pool and in-ground hot tub through large glass windows. The rooms have a modern, hip sensibility, with retro embellishments and custom wood art. All 106 guestrooms and 17 suites underwent renovation in early 2013. The result is retro chic, with leather accents, iPod docking stations, LED lighting, wood floors, fireplaces, and high-definition flat-screen TVs. Bose surround-sound speakers are embedded in the ceilings. The average room is about four hundred square feet. Each room has a small balcony with comfortable outdoor patio seating facing the hills.

**Fess Parker Wine Country Inn** (fessparker.com, 2860 Grand Ave., Los Olivos, 805/688-7788) This inn and spa was built by Fess Parker (a.k.a., Davey Crockett and Daniel Boone in the TV shows), who created a mini-empire that included his own winery. Parker was smart enough to get into real estate after his television days, and he was a fixture of the Valley. This is the only place to stay in Los Olivos; however, Santa Ynez and Solvang are a short drive away. The property has both a wine store and a restaurant. The feel of this traditional inn is changing, pulling in a hipper wine crowd. But it retains the elements people come here for—small-town hospitality, easy access to wine country, and a Victorian Western motif. The rooms are comfortable and large, and they surround a garden courtyard.

**Santa Ynez Inn** (santaynezinn.com, 3627 Sagunto St., 805/688-5588) Visiting this inn is like stepping back into the Victorian era. Think of this as a high-end bed and breakfast and you get the idea. The average room is about six hundred square feet, furnished with nice antiques, and the bathrooms have steam showers and heated tile floors. Breakfast is served each morning in the parlor, a lushly wood-rich Victorian room that feels more museum quality than inn. In the evening the inn offers a wine and cheese reception. There are only twenty rooms here. Walk out your door and you're in Santa Ynez. It's a quiet place in a quiet town to enjoy a quiet experience.

## I Just Won the Lottery

OK, so, if you won the lottery you probably wouldn't be staying around here. There are no high-end properties.

## Planes, Trains, and Automobiles

### Planes

**Santa Maria Airport** (SMX, santamariaairport.com, 805/922-1726) is quite small, but two airlines do fly into here. It might be worth considering if you need a commuter connection from Los Angeles or Las Vegas.

### Trains

Yes, Amtrak cuts through Santa Barbara, but at the coast, not up here—rather ironic considering that the railroad running through the Valley was what made this area.

### Automobiles

Santa Ynez is accessed by Highway 246, which cuts through the area. If you're arriving by car from the north, you can exit and drive through Solvang, or take the

Highway 154 exit and drive the back way. Both drives have their advantages. Driving through Solvang is great if you've never seen the town, but on weekends the road is packed with slow-moving cars, buses, and RVs. The back route can take you

San Marcos Pass, late 1800s. No AC, no phones, no heated seats.

through Los Olivos or along the 154 until you turn right onto Highway 246. This route is all scenic, rolling hills, with some cattle and horses and a few vineyards. If you're driving from the south, take Highway 101 up through the Gaviota Pass and exit through Solvang, or drive the San Marcos Pass, Highway 154, which can also be a long drive depending on traffic. Here you'll pass Cachuma Lake, and chances are you'll see deer and cattle strolling on the oak-studded hillsides.

## Local Resources

The **Santa Ynez Valley Journal** (syvjournal.com) publishes a free, weekly thirty-page newspaper that offers a broad scope of stuff to do around the Valley. The best part, though, is the police blotter, which is more fun to read than anything else. There's also a calendar listing of events and plenty of local stories and interviews.

The **Santa Maria Times** (santamariatimes.com) is the daily paper available throughout Santa Maria. Its rival, the **Santa Maria Sun** (santamariasun.com), is the alternative free weekly published each Thursday. Both focus mainly on Valley issues and parts of southern San Luis Obispo County, less so than the city of Santa Barbara.

The **Lompoc Record** (lompocrecord.com) is a record of the happenings in Lompoc.

STUFF YOU NEED TO KNOW

## AREA CODE

Everything in Santa Barbara County is under the 805 area code. Everything.

## CRIME

Everyone wants to believe that nothing bad will ever befall them on vacation. Uh, yeah, sure. Do your utmost to protect yourself, and be aware and alert when you travel.

- Don't leave your valuables (including your smartphone, iPad, etc.) in plain sight in your car or hotel room.
- Don't flaunt your cash in public. I see this very often— people making a purchase and then walking away with their cash still in hand (ditto at the ATM). Use only well-lighted ATMs in highly public places.
- At night, park under a light, or at the very least in a public place. We have lots of late-night bars and clubs, and walking back to your car parked down a dark alley in a strange city is never a good idea.
- Gang violence is up. Yes, it's true. We've had a few gang problems in broad daylight right on State Street.
- Bank robberies in Santa Barbara average one per month. Surprised? And current trends, according to the FBI, show it increasing. If something is suspicious, call the FBI at 1-888-CANT-HIDE.
- Though cases of dosing someone's drink at a club are uncommon, ladies, keep your drinks and your purse with you at *all* times.

# EARTHQUAKES

I have lived in California all my life and been through many quakes. While you're never sure how severe one will be, panicking is a bad idea. Should a temblor occur while you're visiting, try to remain calm. If you're inside, take cover by getting under a sturdy table (I said sturdy, not a card table) or other piece of furniture and wait until the shaking stops. If there isn't a table or desk near you, cover your face and head with your arms and crouch in an inside corner of the building, where the building supports are strongest. Why? Freestanding, unsupported walls fall easily, that's why. Stay away from glass, windows, exterior doors and walls, and anything that could fall on you, such as lighting fixtures or furniture. Use a doorway for shelter only if it's in close proximity and it's a supported, load-bearing doorway (because I'm sure we all have access to the architectural plans). But seriously, most doorways are reinforced, therefore typically safer. Stay inside until the shaking stops and it's safe to go outside. Research has shown that most injuries occur when people inside build-ings freak out and run outside. Be aware that the electricity may have gone out—as in, no elevators—and the sprin-kler systems or fire alarms may turn on. Do not use the elevators!

If you're outside, move away from buildings, streetlights, and utility wires and wait until the shaking stops. The greatest danger exists directly outside of buildings. Many of the 120 fatalities from the 1933 Long Beach earthquake occurred when people ran outside, only to be killed by falling debris from collapsing walls. Ground movement during an earthquake is seldom the direct cause of death or injury.

If you're driving, stop as quickly as safety permits and stay in the vehicle. Avoid stopping near or under buildings, trees, overpasses, and utility wires. Proceed cautiously once the earthquake has stopped. Avoid roads, bridges, or ramps that might have been damaged by the earthquake.

## HELMET LAWS AND JAYWALKING

Maybe it's the alluring near-perfect weather and sunshine, but so many cyclists ride around without a helmet. Not a good idea. Santa Barbara is very bike friendly, but sharing the roads with cars without being protected is kind of dumb. *California law states that anyone eighteen years of age or younger must wear a helmet.* If you rent a bike, also rent a helmet, or head to a cycle shop and buy one (pun intended). As a cyclist I have many friends, both hardcore cyclists and weekend warriors, who swear their helmets have saved their lives. And please realize it's not just about cars. One friend of mine swerved to avoid hitting a dog and ran into a pole. Someone else I know was going downhill, clipped a rock, and was sent flying off their bike. Helmets do save lives and can prevent serious injuries. At the very least, check out Play It Again Sports (playitagainsports.com), which has stores in Santa Maria and Santa Barbara. It sells used sports equipment, including helmets.

Many people jaywalk (not crossing a street at an appropriate crosswalk). In Santa Barbara, you run the risk of getting a ticket. I've seen it firsthand. Many Europeans cross the street whenever they want, and sure, that's the way it is in Europe. But in Santa Barbara you might find yourself explaining your actions to a police officer.

## HOMELESS

Though the coastal parts of Santa Barbara seem pretty sanitized, we do have a serious issue with the homeless, most noticeably along State Street and along the waterfront in Santa Barbara. There is no easy solution to the problem, but many visitors are shocked at the number of homeless people we have and the aggressive nature of a few of them. I can't tell you what to do with panhandlers; that's your call.

## SALES TAX

Sales tax within the county is 7.75 percent, with the exception of Santa Maria, where it's 8 percent (rebels).

## RESPONSIBLE AND ETHICAL TRAVEL: DON'T BE A DOLT

There is perhaps no greater way to understand ourselves and our world than through the conduit of travel. But with travel comes responsibility: How can we be good travelers and responsible consumers while respecting the environment, the people of the area, and the culture in which we are immersed? Travel is a privilege, not an entitlement. Therefore, when I write about travel or appear as a guest on radio shows, I always encourage a thoughtful approach. I've created a few ideas to help us travel more ethically and responsibly and be better citizens of Planet Earth.

### 1) Minimize Your Environmental Impact

- Ask your hotel if it has a **recycling** program (it should— recycling rates in the US are an abysmal 35 percent; they are much better in Canada and Europe). The morning newspapers, water bottles, and soda cans should be recycled. If the hotel doesn't have a recycling program, suggest it might consider one.
- Recycle yourself: Not you personally. I routinely drink bottled water when I travel because I'm not always certain of the water quality. But I also recycle those bottles at the hotel; if it doesn't have a recycling program, I bring the bottles back with me in my suitcase. Hassle?

199

Nope. The bottles weigh next to nothing and barely take up space. Hint: Put the crumpled bottles inside your shoes.

- Limit your water usage: Many areas around the globe are water-stressed, and this region gets below average rainfall two of every three years. You may be on vacation, but that doesn't mean you need a long shower. Here in Santa Barbara we are prone to bouts of drought.

## 2) Respect All Wildlife

This starts with **not feeding wild animals—any of them!** I know they're cute and curious and you can get close to them, but our own crappy dietary habits include consuming GMOs and artificial ingredients that should not be given to animals; their bodies can't adapt to our unhealthy lifestyles. Feeding animals damages their health, alters their natural behaviors, and exposes them to predators and other dangers. Because humans are at the top of the food chain, *we actually bear a greater responsibility to every other creature* to respect them and treat them well.

## 3) Treat It Like It's Yours

Stay on all designated trails when you hike, bike, and walk. If you camp, camp on durable surfaces and dispose of your garbage properly—especially in parks and most especially if you visit the **Channel Islands**. So, bring a bag with you and pack out exactly what you've packed in. I'm guessing you wouldn't want someone to toss trash on *your* yard, right? Therefore, treat every place you visit like it was your own home. It's easy to think, "I'm on vacation, so I'll do as I please." Well, yeah, I get that idea, but that doesn't mean your vacation is an entitlement.

## 4) Support the Local Economy

I was in Paris to run the Paris Marathon (raising money for cancer research), and part of my group wanted to go to the Hard Rock Café. Mind you, we were in *Paris*, home of the best food anywhere; though the Hard Rock Café employs local Parisians, I can go to a Hard Rock Café anywhere. Visit local places where you can explore and have unique experiences. Supporting local businesses will help the region you visit to thrive. Many places you visit rely on tourism—even here in **Santa Barbara**—and I've seen businesses shut down because visitors shop at chain stores instead of local businesses. Half the fun of traveling is trying new things. I always seek out the local coffee houses, bakeries, breweries, wineries, restaurants, distilleries, shops, and stores.

Ultimately, treat every place you visit like it was your own backyard. My wife and I pick up trash around Santa Barbara, where we live, and we do so everywhere we go, be that Spain, Paris, or China. Trash is trash, and if you can pick up litter on the way to visit a really cool site, you've done a fine thing. So have fun, travel well, learn, and explore; by doing so you will continually evolve into a better person, a truly global soul who ends up being more compassionate, more interesting, and, frankly, more cool to the people you meet.

# YOUR 25 QUESTION QUIZ

## TRUE OR FALSE?

Okay, so you've either read most of this book and have a solid understanding of Santa Barbara County, or you cheated and flipped to this page because you were curious, lazy, or both. Either way, here are twenty-five statements about Santa Barbara. Are they fact or fiction? (Answers on the following pages—no peeking!)

1. Saint Barbara is the patron saint of fish and the protector of architects.

2. The Channel Islands were once part of California but separated from the mainland during a cataclysmic earthquake and tsunami.

3. Santa Barbara is home to one of the oldest buildings in all of California.

4. Santa Barbara used to be referred to as the "Western White House."

5. The wine industry began with the planting of native grapes by the Chumash people near present-day Santa Maria, in what is now the Wal-Mart parking lot.

6. "The Battle of Solvang Hills" was one of the rare instances of West Coast skirmishes during the Civil War.

7. The Santa Barbara Harbor was partially funded by "big yeast" money.

8. Carpinteria was so named by the Spanish because the fields of low-growing scrub brush made the ground look like a carpet.

9. Because of its reputation as a party school, the average four-year graduate degree at UC Santa Barbara takes five years.

10. The name Lompoc Wine Ghetto refers to a county program whereby rehabilitated alcoholics find new life as winemakers.

11. Pop icon Michael Jackson's former home, Neverland Ranch, was originally used to film the big-screen version of Peter Pan.

12. Hidden Valley Ranch dressing was created in Santa Barbara.

13. Many famous couples have honeymooned in Santa Barbara, including future president John F. Kennedy and his new bride, Jackie.

14. Santa Barbara's historic Chinatown eventually disappeared because of the Tong Wars of 1925.

15. In late 2015, Facebook CEO Mark Zuckerberg tried to purchase the historic Montecito fire station to use as a satellite office for Facebook. He was outbid by Oprah Winfrey.

16. More sushi is consumed in Santa Barbara than in any other city in the US.

17. The Vandenberg Air Force Base is home to the little-known "Area 32," where, according to conspiracy theorists, the remnants of a UMO (unidentified marine object) are held in an underground silo.

18. One of the worst US Navy disasters occurred just north of the city of Santa Barbara.

19. Old Mission Santa Barbara is referred to as the "Queen of the Missions" because one night in 1899 local padres consumed too much sacramental wine and things "got out of hand."

20. The 2004 Oscar-winning film *Sideways* about Santa Barbara wine country wasn't even filmed here. It was shot in Malibu.

21. Santa Maria was so named because Spanish missionaries believed they saw an image of Saint Maria in the broccoli fields.

22. In the 1920s, Hollywood film director Cecil B. DeMille actually built the Guadalupe dunes so he could film The Ten Commandments on "real sand."

23. During Spanish rule in Santa Barbara, chocolate was more valuable than gold.

24. Solvang's famed butter cookies achieved international recognition when they were featured on TV's *The Simpsons*.

25. During World War II, Nazis held at local prisons helped harvest grapes for wine.

# ANSWERS

1: False. According to the Catholic Church, Saint Barbara is the patron saint in times of danger from thunderstorms and the protector of artillerymen. It was the city of Santa Barbara that boasted she protected architects.

2: False. The Channel Islands were never part of California, but scientists do believe that the islands, which are visible from the coast, were once one really, really big island called Santarosae.

3: True. El Cuartel, part of the original Presidio, was built in 1782 and is the second-oldest building in the state. Only Mission San Juan Capistrano is older, having been built in 1776.

4: True. When Ronald Reagan was president, his ranch, called Rancho del Cielo, located on Refugio Road, was dubbed the Western White House because he conducted official business here. British Prime Minister Margaret Thatcher and the Soviet Union's Mikhail Gorbachev both visited the ranch.

5: False. It was the Spanish who planted grapes to use for sacramental purposes in the 1790s. The Indians drank pine-needle tea (boring).

6: False. Solvang was founded in 1911, and if that still confuses you about the Civil War I'd advise you to get back to school.

7: True. Max Fleischmann, of Fleischmann's Yeast, ponied up half the money to build the harbor and breakwater, in large part for his large yacht.

8: False. Carpinteria was originally named by the Spanish as "San Roque," allegedly in honor of a French Catholic priest. When Gaspar de Portola's expedition was in town, he saw the abundant tools the industrious Chumash people used, and he thought the area looked like a carpenter's shop—hence, La Carpinteria.

9: False. Though *Surfer Magazine* ranked it one of the top ten surf schools, UCSB is actually one of the top public universities in the nation, offering more than two hundred degrees and credentials.

10: False. But we believe this could be a credible use of taxpayer money.

11: False. While Neverland Ranch is located off Figueroa Mountain Road in the Valley, no movie has ever been filmed there—at least none that we know of.

12: True. Hidden Valley Original ranch dressing was developed in the late 1950s by real ranchers Steve and Gayle Henson. The Hidden Valley Guest Ranch was located off Highway 154.

13: True. They honeymooned at the San Ysidro Ranch in Montecito in 1953.

14: True. When Gin Han was gunned down on Canon Perdido Street in front of two dozen witnesses, it set in motion the end of Chinatown. The killers, however, were never caught.

15: False. Montecito's fire station was never for sale, and Oprah has less money than Zuckerberg, who we believe has no idea where Santa Barbara even is.

16: False. But we're really trying.

17: False. Vandenberg Air Force Base has no "Area 32" . . . that we've ever heard of.

18: True. On Sept. 8, 1923, nine United States Navy destroyers operating at nearly top speed ran onto the rocky reefs of Point Pedernales, known as Honda Point, north of Santa Barbara. Seven of the destroyers sank in forty feet of water, and the disaster resulted in twenty-three deaths.

19: False. There are absolutely no legitimate published reports of this ever happening, nor are there any made-up reports of this happening.

20: False. It was shot all over Santa Barbara.

21: False. I've never heard of this!

22: False. DeMille built the set for *The Ten Commandments*, which he then buried in the dunes.

23: True and false. Cocoa was highly prized, and mission records show how much was requested; once at the mission it was locked up so no one could get to it. Gold, well, gold is still gold.

24: True. In the sixth episode of the nineteenth season, Bart remembers that Millhouse gets Danish butter cookies from Solvang every Christmas. This prompted a lot of people to want to get butter cookies from Solvang.

25. True. Camp Cooke (now known as Vandenberg) had a prison (now the Lompoc Federal Penitentiary) for Italian and German prisoners of war. And yes, they were supervised and put to work on local farms, including walnut orchards, lima bean fields, and vineyards.

# INDEX